Maud Grainger Diehl

Over 400 Favourite Recipes from Families, Friends and Personalities

BACKGROUND

This book and its recipes came into being as a way of providing, under one roof, a "Collection" of unique and treasured recipes from 200 private kitchens.

Some of the 400 recipes have been cherished by grandparents and their families for years; some are completely original; others are simply favourites.

All have been used time and time again, and widely shared among friends.

TO ALL OF YOU THE VERY BEST FROM ALL OF US!

Mrs. William E. Boothe
Mrs. William I. Davies
Mrs. Roberto del Rosal
Miss Janice Gillan
Mrs. Edwin S. Langdon
Mr. Thomas G. Lutton
Mrs. Margaret Marcar
Mrs. Roger W. Matthews
Mrs. James W. McCutcheon
Dr. Robert L. McPhedran
Bev Plaxton
Mrs. William J. Plaxton
Sally Sullivan
Carol Webb

Credits

To the companies who gave their financial assistance, provided the facilities of their offices and lent us their professional staffs, a mere thank you seems inadequate. We are indebted beyond words.

Art Printing Company
Black's Cameras
FBM Distillery Company Limited
F.H. Hayhurst Company Limited
Inter-City Papers Limited
Manor Florists
Mary Maxim Limited
Morris Gay Men's and Women's Fashions
Robin Hood Multifoods Limited
Studio Graphics
Superior Personnel Limited
Willhurst Communications Limited

FIRST PRINTING
October, 1980

Written and published by
EPILEPSY ONTARIO,
Toronto, Canada

Printed by
T.H. BEST PRINTING COMPANY LIMITED

Epilepsy Ontario

Epilepsy Ontario gratefully acknowledges the voluntary assistance, time and assistance of the many people who helped bring this book into being. Without their help and advice, there simply would not have been a book. We could not have managed without them.

When you bought this cookbook, did you realize more was being accomplished than spreading the word for hungry epicures? The entire proceeds will be used to assist those with epilepsy.

A non-profit organization, Epilepsy Ontario was established in 1956 to provide and encourage a multiplicity of programmes and services for those suffering from epilepsy.

The vast majority of you are probably asking at this moment two questions, "What is epilepsy" and "Why are special programmes and services required"?

Epilepsy is not a disease. It is a sign or symptom. It results from, or is part of, an underlying neurological disorder. Seizures may occur at any age to both sexes, to any race, or to any individual.

The second question can best be answered by outlining the following brief facts:

- 2% of the population suffers from a seizure disorder
- the myths and misconceptions associated with epilepsy are often more detrimental to the person with the disorder than the seizures themselves.
- anti-convulsant medication may cost up to $100 a month
- a person with epilepsy is still considered by some to be possessed by a devil or to be retarded
- discrimination in the work force is the most common problem faced by those with epilepsy
- the Human Rights Code does not include persons with epilepsy
- that people with epilepsy pay a higher Life Insurance premium than the general public
- epilepsy is still a "closet" disorder due to discrimination and misconceptions.

We hope you will enjoy the recipes we have given you in this collection. We have enjoyed working on this publication. It has been a joy and a satisfaction.

From the kitchens of:

To all the busy men and women who took time to share their recipes with us go our sincere thanks and gratitude.

Mrs. Tony Allen
Margaret Atwood
Frank Augustyn
Mrs. William Avery
Mrs. J.A. Bacardi
Mrs. Edward Bailey
Mrs. Jean Bally
Mrs. Michael Barber
Mrs. John Barclay
Mrs. W.H. Bartlett
Mrs. W.H. Beale
Mrs. Joseph Berman
Pierre Berton
Patricia Black
Mrs. Alan Blott
Mrs. L. Boland
Mrs. G.W. Bond
Mrs. Edward Boothe
Mrs. William Boothe
Mrs. David Bowden
Bill Brady
Mrs. Ronald Brinkman
Mrs. Logan Brown
Mrs. Victor Burrows
Mrs. C.M. Burton
Café du Midi, London, Ontario
June Callwood
W. Earl Cameron
Mrs. Donald Cannon
Mrs. D.H. Carlisle
Mrs. J. Carraday
Mrs. James Caylor
Mrs. Thomas Chernoff
Zena MacMillan Cherry
Mrs. D.M. Chisholm
Mrs. Lionel Chisholm
Dinah Christie
Mrs. Peter Chubb
Mrs. Eric Clapham
Mrs. J. Cochran
Mrs. Beverly Collombin
Mrs. W.H. Cotton
Mrs. North Cooper
Mrs. R. Cowie
Wally Crouter
Mrs. William Davies
Mrs. T.G. Deacon
Mrs. T.R. Deacon
Mrs. Roberto del Rosal
Mrs. Angelo Delzotto
Mrs. J.M. Dimitrieff
Mrs. J. Dinning
Mrs. Kenneth Duck
Mrs. M.H. Dunlop
Mrs. Paul Eide
Mrs. James Elder
Mrs. G. Enns
Victor Feldbrill
Mrs. Anthony Fell
Mrs. John Finlay
Mrs. A.V. Fleming
Mrs. D. Florence
Maureen Forrester
Four Aces Delicatessen
Mrs. Scott Fowler
Mrs. D'Oliver Frederick
Helen Gagen
Miss Janice Gillan
Mrs. R. Gillan
Clyde Gilmour
Robert Goulet
Mrs. David Hackett
Arthur & Sheila Hailey
Mrs. Warren Hannah
Hagood Hardy
Mrs. Robert Harris
Vanessa Harwood
Mrs. Richard Hastings
Mrs. J. Hilborn
Mrs. J. Hohenadel, Sr.
Mrs. J. Hohenadel
Mrs. Hugh Honsberger
Gordie Howe
Mrs. Charles Hunnisett
Mrs. Frank Hunnisett
Mrs. David Jagger
Mrs. Carl Jellett
Mrs. Frank Johnston
Karen Kain
Mrs. William Kay
Mrs. Timothy Kennish
Mrs. David Kent
Mrs. Allen King
Mrs. E. George Kneider
Moe Koffman
Mrs. William Lamson
Mrs. E. Langdon
Mrs. Brian Laragh
Mrs. Donald Lloyd-Smith
Mrs. Thomas G. Lutton
Mrs. Thomas Lytle
Mrs. Robert Macbeth
Mrs. Sheila MacKay
Mrs. Margaret Marcar
Mrs. Paul Marshall
Cathy Martin
Patrick Martin
Mrs. Roger Matthews
Mrs. Michael Meredith
Miss Marianne Merry
Mrs. Thomas Merry
Mrs. Paul Moffat
Mickie Moore
Mrs. Graham Morrow
Claire & Farley Mowat
Mrs. William Murby
Mrs. L.F. Murphy
Mrs. Philip MacDonnell
Mrs. S. MacMurray
Mrs. James McCutcheon
Giselle Mackenzie
Mrs. Barry McKillop
Mrs. L. McKillop
Ria McMurtry
Mrs. R. McMurtry
Mrs. M. McNab
Mrs. Robert L. McPhedran
Cindy Nicholas
Bobby Orr
Mrs. Larry Pearson
Mrs. Barry Percival
Mrs. Mabel Phillips
Mrs. Alan Plaxton
Mrs. William Plaxton
Mrs. John Stobo Prichard
Liz Primeau
Nancy C. Raine (Greene)
Mrs. M.K. Rawlings
Mrs. Hugh Rennie
Mrs. Neill B. Rewcastle
Mrs. Ian Richards
Mrs. Peter Ridout
Mrs. Edward Ritcey
John J. Robinette, Q.C.
Mr. Paul Romanelli
Etta Sawyer
Mrs. Stephen Secord
Mrs. K. Selby
Mrs. Thomas Shea
Mrs. Murray Shirriff
Frank Shuster
Gord Sinclair
Mrs. J.F. Smith
Mrs. Harland Steele
Bonnie Stern
Mr. Mark A. Sullivan
Mrs. Paul B. Sullivan
Joan Sutton
Lucy Waverman
Mrs. M.M. Williams
Mrs. David Wilson
Cynthia Wine
Mrs. A.R. Winnett
Mrs. Carl Wyse
Mrs. William Yule

Patrons

Our special thanks to our Patrons who so generously enabled us to get a financial start with our first printing.

Mr. and Mrs. Kenneth W. Andras, Jr.
Mr. and Mrs. William W. Andrews
Mr. and Mrs. Ray Arsenault
Mr. and Mrs. David W. Ashworth
Mr. and Mrs. J. Alberto Bacardi
Mr. and Mrs. G. Bascombe
Mr. and Mrs. Douglas A. Berlis
Mr. and Mrs. G.H. Best
Mrs. Marion J. Birch
Patricia Black
Mr. Blair C. Bongard
Mr. and Mrs. A. Edward Boothe
Mr. and Mrs. William E. Boothe
Mr. and Mrs. Logan R. Brown
Mr. and Mrs. A.M. Burka
Mr. and Mrs. J. Barry Burke
Mr. and Mrs. Ronald G. Burrows, Q.C.
Mr. and Mrs. Donald H. Carlisle
Mr. G. Richard Chater
Mr. and Mrs. Thomas Chernoff
Dr. and Mrs. Lionel Chisholm
Mr. and Mrs. G. Blair Cowper-Smith
Mr. and Mrs. R. Gordon Cummings
Dr. R.M. Curtis
Mr. and Mrs. Roberto del Rosal
Mr. and Mrs. Juan L. del Rosal
Mr. and Mrs. J. M. Dimitrieff
Mr. and Mrs. Ian Douglas, Q.C.
Mrs. Margaret H. Dunlap
Dr. and Mrs. John Edmeads
Mr. and Mrs. R. James Elder
Mr. and Mrs. John H. Eliot
Mr. and Mrs. G. English
Mr. and Mrs. Robert Erwin
Mr. Claudius Fehr and Dr. Kevin Fehr
Mr. and Mrs. Albert P. Fell
Mr. and Mrs. Anthony S. Fell
Mr. and Mrs. Charles P. Fell
Mr. and Mrs. Fraser M. Fell
Mr. and Mrs. John R. Finlay
Mr. and Mrs. Douglas Florence
Mr. and Mrs. E. Edward Fry
Mrs. Mary Gordon
Mr. and Mrs. John Guoba
Mr. and Mrs. Peter D.G. Harris
Mr. and Mrs. C.F. Haughton
Mr. W.A. Heaslip
Mr. and Mrs. Vern Heinrichs
Mr. and Mrs. George T. Heintzman
Mrs. Ann M. Hogarth
His Honour Judge Hugh and Mrs. Honsberger
Mrs. Margaret Houlding
Mr. and Mrs. George Ignatieff
Mr. and Mrs. David Kent
Mr. and Mrs. K.W. Kernaghan, Q.C.
Mr. and Mrs. Donald F. King
Mr. and Mrs. E. George Kneider
Mr. and Mrs. Mel Lastman
Mr. and Mrs. Edwin Langdon
Mr. and Mrs. Brian G. Laragh
Mr. and Mrs. Lee Larkin
Dr. and Mrs. Kenneth E. Livingston
Dr. and Mrs. Donald L. Lloyd-Smith
Mr. and Mrs. Thomas G. Lutton
Mrs. Margaret Marcar
Dr. and Mrs. Joseph T. Marotta
Major General A. Bruce Matthews
Mr. and Mrs. Roger W. Matthews
Mr. and Mrs. James W. McCutcheon
Mr. and Mrs. John F. McGarry
Dr. and Mrs. Brian McGrath
Dr. and Mrs. Barry McKillop
Dr. and Mrs. Robert L. McPhedran
Dr. and Mrs. Keith Meloff
Mr. and Mrs. Paul E. Meredith
Miss Marianne Merry
Mr. and Mrs. R.T. Merry
Mr. and Mrs Graham W. Mitchell
Mr. and Mrs. Paul Moffat
Mr. and Mrs. Joseph R. Morris
Pamela Myles
Dr. and Mrs. M. Justin O'Brien
Mr. and Mrs. Fredrick D. O'Connor
Mr. and Mrs. F.D. O'Neill
Mr. and Mrs. G.P. Osler
Mr. and Mrs. Alan D. Plaxton
Mr. and Mrs. William J. Plaxton
Mrs. Susan E. Pollitt
Mr. and Mrs. J.H. Potts, Q.C.
Dr. and Mrs. John Stobo Prichard
Dr. and Mrs. Neill B. Rewcastle
Dr. and Mrs. J. Clifford Richardson
Mr. and Mrs. Hugh Rowan
Mr. and Mrs. Stephen Secord
Mr. and Mrs. Thomas Shea
Mr. Joseph M. Smith
Mr. and Mrs. Alan N. Steiner
Mrs. E.A. Steiner
Dr. and Mrs. Donald A. Stewart
Mr. and Mrs. Ronald Strange
Mr. and Mrs John G.B. Strathy
Mr. and Mrs. R.H. Sturgess
Mr. and Mrs. Paul B. Sullivan
Dr. W. Tucker
Dr. and Mrs. Adrian Upton
Mr. Cameron Wardlaw
Mr. and Mrs. William Williams
Mrs. A.R. Winnett
Dr. and Mrs. Carl W. Wyse

Contents

Appetizers

CHEESE BALL

1-8 ounce package of cream cheese

8 slices smoked beef

1 ½ bunches green onions

1 teaspoon garlic salt

1 tablespoon accent

chopped beef for garnish

Whirl all ingredients in food processor. Shape into a ball. Chill overnight.
Garnish with chopped beef. Serve with melba rounds.

STUFFED SUGAR FIGS

Makes 50

50 dried figs

50 walnut halves

confectioners' sugar

Slightly grease a cookie sheet. Fill figs with walnut halves, pinch closed. Bake at 250° F 10 to 15 minutes. Cool, then roll in confectioners' sugar.
Will keep in an airtight container 1 or 2 weeks.

MELON APPETIZER

Serves 8 to 10

1 medium-sized Persian melon

1 medium-sized Crenshaw melon

2 tablespoons lime juice

2 tablespoons honey

¼ teaspoon each ground coriander and nutmeg

Cut melons in halves, remove and discard seeds. Using melon ball cutter, scoop out all fruit. Place fruit and all juices in a deep bowl.
Mix together lime juice, honey, coriander and nutmeg. Blend with the melon. Cover and chill several hours.
Spoon into serving bowl.

CURRIED HERB DIP

Serves 8

1 cup mayonnaise

½ cup sour cream

1 teaspoon of herb seasoning (either tarragon, basil, parsley or marjoram)

¼ teaspoon salt

¼ teaspoon curry powder

1 tablespoon snipped parsley

1 tablespoon grated onion

1 ½ teaspoons lemon juice

½ teaspoons Worcestershire sauce

Mix all ingredients together. Serve with small raw vegetable pieces of broccoli, cauliflower, carrots, celery, raw mushrooms, or cherry tomatoes.

Always popular!

MUSHROOM SPREAD (or FILLING)

Serves 6 to 8

½ pound mushrooms

2 tablespoons butter

1 medium onion, chopped

½ teaspoon salt

freshly ground pepper

dash of nutmeg (or grating of fresh)

1 teaspoon lemon juice

2 teaspoons flour

½ cup sour cream

½ to 1 teaspoon dill

Trim mushrooms and wipe clean. Chop finely. Heat butter in skillet, add mushrooms and onions; cook briskly for 4 minutes, stirring. Sprinkle with salt and pepper, nutmeg, lemon juice, and flour. Cook 1 to 2 minutes more. Remove from heat; add sour cream and dill.

Super spread on pumpernickel! May be used as filling in miniature tart shells.

SEAFOOD STUFFED MUSHROOMS

Makes 30 to 40 Mushroom Caps

2 pounds large mushrooms

1-7½ ounce can crabmeat, drained

1-7½ ounce can shrimps, drained

1-8 ounce package cream cheese, softened

1 cup shredded Swiss cheese

salt, pepper and paprika to taste

Clean and remove stems from mushrooms. In a deep dish, clean and dice crabmeat and shrimps. Add cream cheese, salt and pepper to taste and a sprinkle of paprika.

Stuff mixture into mushroom caps. Sprinkle with shredded Swiss cheese. Bake at 350°F for 10 to 15 minutes.

BAKED STUFFED MUSHROOMS

Makes 12 Mushroom Appetizers

12 large mushrooms

3 tablespoons butter

1 tablespoon chopped green onions

1 ½ tablespoons flour

¼ cup chicken stock or sherry or cream or red wine

grating of nutmeg

1 tablespoon of chopped parsley, fresh

salt and pepper to taste

6 crackers, crushed

2 tablespoons melted butter

Wash mushrooms and pat dry. Remove stems and chop finely. In a heavy skillet, melt butter; sauté onions and chopped mushroom stems, cook slowly for 10 minutes. Add flour and liquid of your choice; mix well. Add nutmeg, parsley, salt and pepper. Cool.

Put mushroom caps in buttered dish; fill with mixture; cover with mixture of cracker crumbs and melted butter. Heat for 15 minutes at 425°F.

HELEN GAGEN'S CRAB DIABLE PUFFS

Makes 18 to 24 Puffs

2½ tablespoons butter

1 medium-sized onion, finely chopped

½ green pepper, finely chopped

1 rib celery, fine chopped

1 teaspoon curry powder

1 teaspoon dry mustard

½ teaspoon salt

freshly ground black pepper

generous dash cayenne

1½ tablespoons flour

6 ounces frozen snow crab, thawed, drained and flaked

1 to 1½ teaspoons Worcestershire sauce

paprika to taste

tiny baked cream puff shells

Melt butter and in it cook onion, pepper and celery, until onion is translucent. Mix in curry powder, mustard, salt, pepper and cayenne. Cook and stir gently for 2 minutes.

Remove from heat; blend in flour and stir in cream. Stir, while heating, until mixture reaches boiling point and thickens. Add crab, Worcestershire sauce and paprika. Stir, then heat until mixture boils. Season to taste. If mixture is too thick, stir in a little more cream.

To serve, spoon the crab mixture into small cream puff shells and bake in 350°F oven until heated through.

Recipe makes 1¾ cups of filling.

EASY PATÉ

Serves 6 to 8

½ tablespoon gelatine (more in summertime!)

1-10 ounce can beef condensed consommé

2 ounces brandy

1-4 ounce package cream cheese, softened

2-3 ounce cans liver paté

1 clove garlic, crushed

salt and pepper to taste

parsley for garnish

In a saucepan, sprinkle gelatine over consommé and heat until gelatine dissolves. Add brandy. Pour into a loaf pan, about ¼ inch deep; reserve remaining consommé. Chill until very firm.

Mix remaining ingredients until very smooth. Spread over chilled consommé. Cool reserved consommé until it reaches consistency of egg white; pour over liver paté and chill overnight. Unmould and decorate with parsley.

Serve with toast triangles.

EASY LIVER PATÉ

Serves 6

1½ packages unflavoured gelatine

3 tablespoons water

1-10 ounce can condensed consommé

1 Braunschweiger liver sausage, at room temperature

1½ teaspoons mayonnaise

2 tablespoons vinegar

2 tablespoons finely chopped onion

parsley or watercress for garnish

Dissolve gelatine in 3 tablespoons water. Heat consommé in a saucepan; add dissolved gelatine. Pour into an oiled, deep bowl (about 6 inches in diameter). Refrigerate until set.

In a medium-sized bowl, mash Braunschweiger sausage; add mayonnaise, vinegar, and onions. With a large spoon, scoop a "well" in the jellied consommé, leaving a consommé lining in the bowl ½ inch all around. Put the scooped out jellied consommé in a small saucepan; heat to liquefy.

Fill the "well" with liver paté mixture. Pour heated consommé over liver paté. Refrigerate until set. Turn out onto a serving plate and garnish with parsley or watercress.

CUCUMBER CAVIAR

Serves 8 to 10

2 medium cucumbers, peeled, seeded and chopped

1 teaspoon salt

1/4 cup olive oil

1/2 cup chopped onions

1 medium tomato, peeled, seeded and chopped

1 clove of garlic, crushed

1 tablespoon lemon juice

1/2 teaspoon salt

1/4 teaspoon pepper

Sprinkle cucumber with salt and let stand about 20 minutes with the weight of a plate on top. Drain. Rinse cucumber in cold water and pat thoroughly dry.

Heat oil in frying pan. Cook gently, cucumber, onions, tomato and garlic, stirring occasionally, until moisture is nearly evaporated. Stir in lemon juice, salt and pepper. Chill. Serve on melba rounds or crisp rye wafers.

Elegance with a difference!

ARTICHOKE HEART SQUARES

Makes 20 Squares

2-6 ounce tins artichoke hearts, packed in oil

1 onion, chopped

1 clove garlic, chopped

4 eggs

1/8 teaspoon pepper

1/8 teaspoon oregano

few grains cayenne

1/4 teaspoon salt

1/4 cup bread crumbs

1/2 pound Cheddar cheese, grated

2 tablespoons parsley

Drain one of the jars of artichokes. Drain second jar into a frying pan, sauté onion and garlic. Take all artichokes, onion and garlic and put into a processor; mix well. Press into 3 inch x 8 inch greased pan. Bake at 325°F for 30 to 35 minutes.

Allow to stand for 5 minutes before cutting into squares and serving.

STUFFED MUSHROOMS

Makes 15 to 20 Caps

1 pound mushroom caps

4 ounces cream cheese

1/3 cup Parmesan cheese

1 clove garlic, minced

dash of Worcestershire sauce

Wash and pat dry mushrooms thoroughly. Mix remaining ingredients. Fill mushroom caps with mixture. Place caps on lightly greased cookie sheet. Bake at 350°F for 15 to 20 minutes.

Your kids can do this one for you!

MUSHROOM CROUSTADES

Serves 12

1 loaf white bread, sliced

2 tablespoons soft butter

1/4 cup butter

3 tablespoons finely chopped shallots

1/2 pound mushrooms, finely chopped

2 tablespoons flour

1 cup heavy cream

1/2 teaspoon salt

1/8 teaspoon cayenne

1 tablespoon chopped parsley

1 tablespoon chopped chives

1/2 teaspoon lemon juice

3 tablespoons grated Parmesan cheese

Cut 3 inch rounds from each slice of bread. Coat the inside of muffin tins with soft butter. Fit rounds into tins and bake at 400°F for 10 minutes or until lightly browned. Remove and cool. (can be done day before, store in an airtight container). Melt 1/4 cup butter. Sauté shallots over medium heat for 3 minutes. Stir in mushrooms and cook 10 to 15 minutes until moisture has evaporated. Sprinkle flour over mushrooms and stir. Add cream, all at once; bring to a boil, lower heat and simmer until thickened.

Add salt, cayenne, parsley, chives and lemon juice. This can be done ahead and refrigerated until ready to use.

Fill each croustade with mushroom filling, sprinkle with cheese and place on a cookie sheet. Heat in oven 350°F for 10 minutes. Serve hot.

Always a winner!

W. EARL CAMERON'S MIDNIGHT PARTY SANDWICH

Serves 12

1-12 ounce can cold meat, ham, corned beef, etc

1/2 pound sharp Cheddar cheese

2 hard-cooked eggs

1/3 cup chopped green onion

3 tablespoons mayonnaise

1/2 cup chili sauce

12 hamburger buns

Chop together cold meat, cheese, eggs and onions. Stir in mayonnaise, and chili sauce.

Spread mixture on bottom half of buns, and cover with top half. Wrap in foil. Heat in 450°F oven for 15 to 20 minutes. Serve hot.

May be frozen

A "newsworthy" recipe.

COCKTAIL MEATBALLS

1 pound ground chuck

½ cup bread crumbs

¼ cup milk

1 tablespoon chopped onion

salt and pepper to taste

Mix above ingredients; shape into small balls. Sauté in butter until dark brown on all sides.

Sauce:

1 cup sherry

1 cup ketchup

½ teaspoon oregano

pinch garlic powder

Mix all ingredients. Add meatballs. Simmer meatballs in sauce for 20 minutes.
Serve with toothpicks.

APPETIZER MEATBALLS

Serves 35

This recipe makes about 75 small bite-sized meatballs. Mix and shape the balls well ahead of time. You can cook these ahead, freeze; and when you need them, place them, thawed, in a double boiler with sweet and sour sauce to heat.

¾ cup soya sauce

¾ cup water

2 small cloves garlic, crushed

2 teaspoons ground ginger

3 pounds ground chuck beef

Sweet and Sour sauce

Combine soya sauce, water, garlic and ginger; mix until blended. Add chuck beef and blend lightly, but thoroughly. Form one inch meatballs and arrange in a large baking pan. Cook at 275°F, uncovered, for about 15 minutes. Turn once during the baking time. These may be served in a chafing dish mixed with sweet and sour sauce or with sauce as a dip.

Serve with toothpicks.

SALMON LOG

1-7¾ ounce can salmon

1-8 ounce package cream cheese

1 tablespoon lemon juice

2 teaspoons minced onion

1 teaspoon horseradish

¼ teaspoon salt

1 teaspoon liquid smoke

½ cup chopped walnuts

3 tablespoons chopped parsley

Blend all ingredients, except walnuts and parsley in food processor or mix well. Refrigerate. Roll in mixture of walnuts and parsley to make a log.

Note: Liquid Smoke is available at Ziggy's

SALMON PATÉ

Serves 10 to 12

1-15½ ounce can salmon

1-8 ounce package cream cheese

1 tablespoon lemon juice

1 teaspoon horseradish

¼ teaspoon salt

¼ teaspoon Tabasco

¼ teaspoon Worcestershire sauce

1 teaspoon grated onion

1 tablespoon chopped fresh parsley

½ tablespoon chopped pecans, optional

In a food processor, or blender, blend all ingredients, except salmon and nuts, for 1 minute. Add salmon and blend for 2 minutes more. Stir in nuts. Chill and serve with crackers.

CHICKEN LIVER PATE NO. 1

Serves 8 to 10

1 cup finely chopped onion

1 cup butter

1 pound chicken livers

1 small bay leaf

1 teaspoon salt

½ teaspoon each of oregano, pepper and thyme

1 tablespoon butter, softened

2 tablespoons brandy, scotch or rye

Sauté onions in butter until browned; remove with a slotted spoon and reserve.

To the skillet with drippings, add chicken livers, bay leaf, salt, oregano, pepper and thyme. Sauté until chicken livers are brown but still pink in the middle.

Discard the bay leaf. In the blender, blend onions and chicken liver mixture until smooth. Stir in butter and liquor. Blend again; then chill.

Serve with melba rounds.

SHRIMP PATÉ

Serves 12

1 tablespoon unflavoured gelatine (1 envelope)

1 cup chicken broth

salt and pepper to taste

pinch of ginger

¼ cup finely chopped shallots

¾ pound cooked, shelled shrimp

¼ cup mayonnaise

2 tablespoons lemon juice

1 cup 35% cream

Soften gelatine in a small amount of broth. In a small pan mix gelatine, broth, spices and shallots and cook until gelatine is dissolved and shallots soft.

In food processor fitted with steel blade, process above mixture, shrimps, mayonnaise and lemon juice until smooth. Refrigerate until syrupy.

Whip cream into soft peaks and fold into shrimp mixture. Pour into mould and refrigerate overnight. Unmould, garnish with fresh shrimp.

Serve with melba toast or pumpernickel bread.

HOT CRAB (OR LOBSTER)

Serves 10 to 12

1 pound Velveeta cheese

½ pound butter

1-15 ounce can crabmeat (or lobster)

In the top of a double boiler melt together cheese and butter. When melted, stir in crabmeat. Serve warm in a chafing dish. This must be kept warm while serving.

Perfect with Triscuits.

Quick. Easy! Delicious!

MUSHROOM APPETIZERS IN PHYLLO PASTRY

Serves 16 to 18

¼ cup butter

1 medium onion, finely chopped

1 pound mushrooms, sliced

salt and pepper to taste

2 tablespoons Madeira

1 to 2 tablespoons fresh dill, finely chopped

2 tablespoons fresh parsley, finely chopped

¾ cup sour cream

½ pound commercial Phyllo pastry

½ cup butter, melted and warm

dry bread crumbs

Preheat oven to 375°F. Melt ¼ cup butter and sauté onion until soft. Add mushrooms and stir together. Add Madeira and seasonings; cook down until most of liquid evaporates. Let cool. Stir in sour cream.

Use 1 phyllo sheet at a time and cover the rest with a damp tea towel to prevent drying. Cut each sheet lengthwise into strips 3 inches wide and brush with the melted butter. Sprinkle with bread crumbs.

Place a spoonful of mushroom filling at one end and fold upwards into a triangle shape. Press edges to seal well. Repeat until all filling is used (or you can just eat the filling!)

Place triangles on a cookie sheet. Brush with butter. Bake 20 minutes at 350°F or until triangles are golden brown and have puffed. These freeze well before cooking.

MUSHROOM ROLLS

Makes 48 Rolls

2 tablespoons butter

1/2 pound mushrooms, finely chopped

1 1/2 tablespoons lemon juice

1 tablespoon flour

1/2 cup light cream

2 tablespoons chopped chives

1 large loaf thinly sliced white bread

In a skillet melt butter and sauté mushrooms until well-browned. Add lemon juice; stir in flour, then cream. Cook, stirring, until slightly thick. Add chives. Allow to cool.

Remove crusts from bread and with a rolling pin, roll each slice until quite thin. Spread on mushroom mixture; roll up; cut in half; refrigerate until party time. Bake on a cookie sheet in a 350°F oven for 10 to 15 minutes, turning once.

SNAIL STUFFED MUSHROOM CAPS

Makes 24 Caps

2 dozen canned snails, drained

2 dozen mushroom caps

6 medium garlic cloves

2 inch celery stalk

handful fresh parsley

1/2 pound butter, cut in 1 inch cubes

black pepper to taste

1 tablespoon lemon juice

2 tablespoons fine bread crumbs

Rinse snails and pat dry. Wipe mushroom caps.

In food processor, fitted with steel blade, chop garlic, celery and parsley. Add to machine, while running, butter. Using on-off method, process juice and crumbs with butter mixture.

Place a snail in each cap and cover with butter mixture. Bake at 400°F for 15 minutes. Serve with French bread.

RIA MCMURTRY'S CHEESIES

Makes 3 dozen Cheesies

8 ounces Imperial cheese

½ cup butter

1 cup flour

2 cups Rice Krispies

½ teaspoon salt

dash of Tabasco

dash of Worcestershire

Soften cheese and butter; mix very well. Mix in flour and seasonings. Stir in Rice Krispies; mix and chill. Roll into balls. On a cookie sheet, flatten each ball with a fork, about 1 inch apart.

Bake at 350°F for 15 minutes.

SPICED PEANUTS

Serves 6

1 egg white

1 1/2 cups salted peanuts

1/2 cup white sugar

1 teaspoon cinnamon

Combine egg white with 1 teaspoon water and beat until frothy. Add nuts, sugar and cinnamon and stir until nuts are well coated.

Spread in lightly oiled roasting pan and roast at 250° F (120° C.) for one hour. Stir every 20 minutes. Let cool in pan, stirring occasionally.

ANTIPASTO

Makes 1 Quart

1-4 ounce can pimientos, drained and chopped

3 green peppers, chopped

1/4 cup vegetable oil

1-7 ounce can tuna fish

1/2 cup vinegar

1-10 ounce can sliced mushrooms, drained

1 cup sweet mixed pickles, chopped

1 dozen stuffed olives, sliced

1 dozen pitted ripe olives, sliced

1 cup ketchup

1 cup bottled chili sauce

2 garlic cloves, crushed

pinch of cinnamon

1 bay leaf

Sauté pimientos and peppers in oil for 10 minutes. Add remaining ingredients. Simmer 10 minutes. Remove bay leaf.

Bottle. Refrigerate, for at least 8 days before using. Serve with crackers. Especially good with poppy seed crackers.

An excellent "starter."

TUNA DIP

Serves 6 to 8

1-7 ounce can solid white tuna, drained and flaked

1-8 ounce package cream cheese, softened

2 tablespoons chili sauce

1 tablespoon onion flakes

2 tablespoons minced parsley

Tobasco to taste

Blend thoroughly the above ingredients. Serve with melba rounds or vegetable pieces.

MEDALLIONS OF MOZZARELLA

Mozzarella cheese

flour

1 egg, well beaten

bread crumbs

Cut medallions (size of a 50 cent piece, ½ inch thick) of cheese. Roll each piece of cheese in flour, then egg, then bread crumbs. Deep-fry in olive oil (¼ inch of oil in a heavy skillet) until golden brown on both sides.

A superb appetizer.

"CAVIAR" PIE

Serves 12

2-8 ounce packages cream cheese, softened

1-1 ounce jar black caviar (lumpfish)

6 hard-cooked eggs, separated and chopped

6 green onions, chopped

1-4 ounce jar black caviar (lumpfish)

½ cup finely chopped parsley

toast triangles or melba rounds

Spread dinner-sized plate completely with cream cheese. Beginning in the centre, mound red caviar. Surround that with chopped egg yolks; then chopped onions; then black caviar, then chopped egg whites. At this point you should have worked your way to the edge of the plate. Then, sprinkle the parsley completely around the edge of the plate.

Serve with toast triangles; slice bread and remove crusts; toast.

Terrific to look at and divine.

MUSHROOM TART HORS D'OEUVRES

Serves 12

½ pound mushrooms

¼ pound butter

1 bunch green onions

handful of fresh parsley

salt and pepper to taste

1-4 ounce package cream cheese

Filling:

In food processor, fitted with steel blade, finely chop mushrooms, onions and parsley. Sauté this mixture in butter, season with salt and pepper; stir in cream cheese until melted. Refrigerate overnight.

Use mushroom mixture to fill baked tart shells and heat or on bread for rolled hot sandwich rolls. Mixture superb in omelettes or added to gravies.

Very versatile!

MARINATED MUSHROOMS

Serves 6 to 8

1 ½ pounds large mushrooms

1 small onion, finely chopped

2 shallots, finely chopped

2 tablespoons finely chopped chives

chopped parsley for garnish

buttered dark bread

Trim mushrooms and break off stems. Thinly slice caps and stems. Combine in a bowl with onions, shallots and chives.

Marinade:

⅔ cup olive oil

¼ cup tarragon vinegar

¼ cup white wine

1 garlic clove, crushed

1 tablespoon grated lemon rind

In a small bowl, combine olive oil, tarragon vinegar and white wine. Add a crushed garlic clove and grated lemon rind. Whisk the mixture until well blended.

Pour the marinade over mushrooms and chill for 1 hour or until they are wilted. Toss them gently several times. Sprinkle mushrooms with chopped parsley. Serve with thin slices of buttered dark bread.

HELEN GAGEN'S GINGER FRUIT CHEESE BALL

Serves 8

1 1/2 pounds white cream cheese, softened

1/4 to 1/3 cup preserved ginger, drained and chopped

1/4 cup crushed pineapple, drained

2 tablespoons maraschino cherries, drained and chopped

toasted slivered almonds, filberts or cashews, chopped

Combine cheese, ginger, pineapple and cherries; shape as a ball. Wrap in plastic and refrigerate until the ball just holds its shape. Roll cheese in nuts, re-shaping if necessary. Makes a ball a little over 4 inches in diameter. Refrigerate until about 30 minutes before serving.

Surround on serving plate with assorted crisp crackers.

Note: If the ball is made ahead, roast almonds in a little butter and drain on absorbent paper before rolling the ball in them. Ginger may be increased, or omit pineapple and cherries and use 3/4 cup ginger.

HOT CREAMED CRAB AND CHEESE

Serves 8

1-8 ounce package cream cheese

1-7 ounce can flaked crabmeat

Worcestershire sauce to taste

Tabasco to taste

1 tablespoon sour cream

1 tablespoon white vine vinegar

salt to taste

Parmesan cheese, grated

Mix first seven ingredients together and put in a small baking dish or two ramekins. Sprinkle with Parmesan cheese. Bake at 350°F for 1/2 hour.

Serve with melba rounds.

Marvelous appetizer.

LOBSTER OR CRABMEAT FANCIES

Makes approximately 36 Fancies

1/2 cup butter

1/2 pound processed cheese

2-5 ounce cans lobster, drained and flaked

1/4 teaspoon salt

1/8 teaspoon pepper

1 Sandwich loaf, thinly sliced

melted butter

Melt butter and cheese in double boiler. Add lobster, salt and pepper to melted cheese mixture. Cut crusts from bread slices; roll slightly to flatten. Spread with lobster mixture. Roll up. Freeze.

When ready to use, cut each roll in half; spread with melted butter. Bake in 400°F oven for 15 minutes.

Make more than you think you will need; these disappear very quickly.

Soups and Salads

WHITE GAZPACHO

Serves 4 to 6

2 cups chicken stock or broth

1 ½ cups chopped watercress

2 medium cucumbers, peeled and sliced

1 medium green pepper, seeded and sliced

3 tablespoons fresh chopped dill

2 tablespoons chopped scallions

3 tablespoons mayonnaise

3 tablespoons sour cream

3 tablespoons white wine vinegar

2 tablespoons sugar

1 teaspoon salt

½ teaspoon pepper

In a blender purée the chicken stock, watercress, cucumbers, green pepper, dill and scallions. Add mayonnaise, sour cream, vinegar, sugar, salt and pepper. Blend until smooth. Chill for 3 hours.

Before serving garnish with chopped dill.

CHILLED LEEK AND WATERCRESS SOUP

Serves 8

1 ½ cups well washed minced leeks

1 cup minced onions

1 crushed garlic clove

¼ cup butter

2 potatoes, peeled and thinly sliced

1 ½ bunches watercress, coarsely chopped

3 cups chicken stock

1 cup milk

1 cup cream

Sauté in ¼ cup butter until translucent but not browned (about 20 minutes), 1 ½ cups minced leeks, 1 cup minced onions, 1 crushed garlic clove.

Add 2 potatoes, peeled and thinly sliced, 1 ½ bunches watercress, coarsely chopped, 3 cups chicken stock. Simmer for 25 minutes.

Press the above mixture through a sieve. Add 1 cup milk and 1 cup cream. Chill. Garnish with a sprig of watercress.

BILL BRADY'S CANADIAN CHEDDAR CHEESE SOUP

Serves 4

4 tablespoons chopped onion

¼ cup diced celery

¼ cup diced carrots

4 tablespoons butter

2 tablespoons flour

1½ cups chicken stock

2½ cups milk

3 cups grated Canadian Cheddar cheese

½ cup beer

croutons for garnish

chopped parsley for garnish

Sauté the vegetables in the butter until softened. Add the flour, blending well and cook for about a minute. Add the chicken stock and cook, stirring constantly, until thickened. Add milk and heat through but do not boil. Strain and return to heat. Add 3 cups of grated cheese and blend until all cheese is melted. Adjust seasonings if necessary. Just before serving add the beer and reheat to serving temperature.

Garnish with croutons, chopped parsley or both.

AVOCADO SOUP

Serves 4 to 6

1 teaspoon butter

1 teaspoon curry powder

2 cups water

1 envelope chicken noodle dry soup mix

1 teaspoon lemon juice

dash Worcestershire sauce

2 ripe avocados, peeled

1 cup light cream

1 cup milk

Melt butter with curry and add water and chicken noodle soup mix. Bring to a boil; then simmer 7 minutes.

Cool.

Add lemon juice and dash of Worcestershire sauce.

Pour the above into blender. Add ripe avocados, cream and milk. Blend until smooth. Refrigerate several hours.

Easy, and a conversation piece.

ORANGE - CARROT SOUP

Serves 6

2 tablespoons butter

½ teaspoon freshly minced ginger

1 pound thinly sliced carrots (about 6)

½ cup sliced leeks (whites only)

3 cups chicken broth

1½ cups fresh orange juice

dash salt, white pepper

orange slices

grated raw carrot

Melt butter in saucepan. Add ginger, carrots and leeks. Sauté until leeks are soft. Add 2 cups of chicken broth, cover and simmer until carrots are cooked, about 30 minutes.

Whirl in blender; return to saucepan. Add remaining chicken broth and enough orange juice to desired consistency. Season to taste. Chill. Top with orange slices and grated carrot.

Delicious served hot or cold.

LEMON SOUP

Serves 6

6 cups chicken broth

¼ cup long grain rice

1 teaspoon salt

3 eggs

¼ cup fresh lemon juice

1 lemon, thinly sliced

In a large saucepan, combine chicken broth, rice and salt. Bring to a boil, cover, reduce heat and simmer until rice is tender. Remove pan from heat.

In a bowl beat eggs until fluffy. Beat in lemon juice. Slowly stir 2 cups of hot broth into egg-lemon mixture and whisk vigourously. Pour this mixture back into saucepan. Whisk again. Cool to room temperature; refrigerate until very cold. Garnish with lemon slices just before serving.

CUCUMBER VICHYSOISSE

Serves 6 to 8

1 pound new potatoes

2 ounces butter

1 small onion, chopped

2 pints chicken broth

1 cucumber, skin on

1 teaspoon sugar

¼ pint thin cream

salt and white pepper to taste

Cut the potatoes in pieces, unpeeled. Sauté butter and onion in large saucepan for 10 minutes. Add potatoes, broth and cucumber.

Bring to a boil and simmer 15 to 20 minutes.

Process, either in food processor or blender until smooth. Add sugar and season with salt and white pepper to taste. Cool, then stir in cream. Chill.

To serve hot, omit cream.

HEAT AND EAT SOUP

Serves 6

1-10 ounce can condensed mushroom soup

1-10 ounce can condensed asparagus soup

1-5 ounce can crabmeat (drained)

2 cups light cream

¼ cup sherry

Mix. Heat. Enjoy!
A great taste.

TANTE RITA'S VEGETABLE SOUP

Serves 10 to 12

4 tablespoons butter

4 tablespoons olive oil

1 medium-sized turnip, peeled and chopped

8 medium-sized carrots, sliced

1 bunch celery, chopped

6 medium-sized onions, chopped

2 tablespoons sugar

2 teaspoons salt

2 tablespoons poultry seasoning

4 tablespoons chopped parsley

1 tablespoon pepper

2 tablespoons chopped chives

6 tablespoons consommé, undiluted (or 6 beef cubes)

2-19 ounce cans tomatoes

In a large pot, sauté vegetables gently in butter and olive oil. Add remaining ingredients and enough water to cover vegetables. Simmer soup, uncovered, until vegetables are tender. Serve with hot rolls.
A meal in itself!

1

Tante Rita's Vegetable Soup
Recipe on page 32

SUMMERTIME SOUP

Serves 6

2 cups buttermilk

4 green shallots or scallions, cut into 1 inch pieces

¼ green pepper, seeded and cut into 3 pieces

1-10 ounce can condensed tomato soup

¼ teaspoon Worcestershire sauce

2 or 3 drops Tabasco

½ teaspoon salt

sour cream for topping

Measure all ingredients except the sour cream into the blender container. Cover and blend for 30 seconds. Chill until icy cold and serve in chilled soup dishes. Garnish with 1 teaspoon sour cream.

CURRIED SCALLOP BISQUE

Serves 4 to 6

1 tablespoon butter

½ teaspoon curry powder

1½ teaspoons grated onion

1-10 ounce can condensed tomato soup

2 cups chicken stock or broth

1 pound scallops

1 cup milk

½ cup cream

½ teaspoon salt

⅛ teaspoon pepper

2 tablespoons snipped parsley

In a small saucepan melt butter; add curry powder and onion. Cook gently, stirring for 3 minutes.

Add tomato soup and chicken stock. Bring to a boil.

Add washed scallops (halved if large). Reduce heat and cook, covered for 5 minutes.

Stir in milk, cream, salt and pepper. Heat through but do not boil. Stir in parsley and serve immediately.

CRABBY CREAM SOUP

Serves 4

1-10 ounce can condensed cream of mushroom soup

1-10 ounce can condensed cream of asparagus soup

1 cup milk

1-7½ ounce can crabmeat

1 teaspoon Worcestershire sauce

3 tablespoons sherry

½ cup whipping cream

Heat soups and milk together. Add crabmeat and Worcestershire. Stir in sherry and whisk gently. Stir in whipping cream. Heat through.

Always a crowd pleaser!

CRAB OR MUSSEL CHOWDER

Serves 4 to 6

1 green pepper, chopped

¼ pound salt pork or ham, diced

1 large onion, chopped

1 celery stalk, chopped

2 medium potatoes, diced

1 small bay leaf (optional)

2 cups water

salt and pepper to taste

2 ¼ cups milk

2 tablespoons flour

1-9 ounce can cooked mussels, or 1-5 ounce can crabmeat drained,

1 tablespoon chopped parsley for garnish

Blanche green pepper by cooking in boiling water for 1 minute; drain. Rinse under cold water and drain again. In large saucepan, fry pork over gentle heat, stirring until it starts to brown. Add onion and celery, cook until golden brown. Add green pepper, potatoes, bay leaf and water and bring to a boil. Season and simmer 10 minutes or until potatoes are tender. Remove from heat.

Gradually add ½ cup milk to flour, stirring to form a smooth mixture; blend into chowder. Return to heat and stir until boiling. Heat remaining milk; add to chowder with the mussels or crab. Simmer 4 to 5 minutes before serving.

Scatter a little parsley over the soup in each serving bowl.

ARTHUR & SHEILA HAILEY'S APPLE SOUP

Serves 2 generously

1 apple

1 medium onion

salt to taste

1-10 ounce can consommé, undiluted

1 pint 18% cream

1 tablespoon scotch whisky

or

1 tablespoon curry

Quarter apple and take out core. Do not peel. Place in top of double boiler. Add peeled, quartered onion. Pour undiluted consommé over them. Cover and simmer over hot water until apple is very soft. Strain.

When ready to serve add cream and heat to boiling point. Add whisky or curry and serve at once.

OYSTER-SPINACH BISQUE

Serves 6 to 8

1 pint oysters (may be frozen)

½ cup of spinach (may be frozen)

2 tablespoons butter

2 tablespoons flour

1 cup milk

salt, pepper and cayenne to taste

whipped cream for topping

Simmer spinach until most of the juice is gone. Combine oysters, spinach, butter, flour and milk in blender. Blend until smooth. Season with salt, pepper and cayenne to taste. This much may be done ahead. Heat and pour into soup cups. Top with whipped cream and brown under broiler, being careful to watch constantly.

CHILLED SPINACH AND CUCUMBER SOUP

Serves 6 to 8

1 bunch green onions, sliced

2 tablespoons butter

4 cups peeled, diced English cucumber

3 cups chicken broth

1-10 ounce package frozen spinach

½ cup peeled, sliced potatoes

1 teaspoon salt

tarragon to taste

lemon juice to taste

pepper to taste

1 cup light cream

Sauté onion in butter. Add all remaining ingredients except cream. Simmer until potatoes are tender.

Whirl in blender. Add cream and chill.

Serve with sliced cucumbers.

A summer's delight.

A MEAL OF SOUP

Serves 4

1-7 ounce can crabmeat, drained

1-10 ounce can condensed consommé, undiluted

2-10 ounce cans condensed tomato soup

1-10 ounce can condensed pea soup

1 jigger sherry

salt and pepper to taste

1 teaspoon Worcestershire sauce

Soak crabmeat in consommé for 1 hour. Mix tomato and pea soups with equal parts milk. Heat soup mixture and add seasonings; stir in crabmeat with consommé and heat thoroughly.

BLOODY MARY SOUP

Serves 4

2 tablespoons butter

1 medium-sized onion, finely chopped

3 sticks of celery, diced

2 tablespoons tomato paste

1 tablespoon sugar

garlic (optional)

5 cups tomato juice

1 tablespoon salt

2 teaspoons Worcestershire sauce

¼ teaspoon pepper

dash of lemon juice

4 tablespoons vodka

sour cream for garnish

Melt butter and gently fry onion and celery until golden brown. Stir in tomato paste, sugar and garlic. Add tomato juice and simmer for ten minutes.

Add remaining ingredients. Liquidize in blender. May be served hot or cold. Garnish with a dollop of sour cream.

For a brunch with a difference.

CHILLED ARTICHOKE SOUP

Serves 4 to 6

1-14 ounce can artichokes

1/2 teaspoon basil

salt and white pepper to taste

1 cup light cream

1 tablespoon chopped chives (additional chopped chives for garnish)

Blend artichokes, a couple at a time so as not to clog the blender. Add remaining ingredients and blend well. Chill thoroughly. Top each soup cup with chopped chives before serving.

MILLER HOWE CREAM SOUPS

Provided you use the basic butter and onions, you may use 2 pounds of any FRESH vegetable and make the soup of your choice.

Here are some ideas:

Carrot (2 pounds) and Coriander (2 tablespoons of coriander seeds).

Turnip (2 pounds) and Dill (1 tablespoon of dill seeds).

Zucchini (1 pound) and Fennel (1 pound).

Brussels sprouts (2 pounds) and when blended add 4 ounces ground hazelnuts.

Peanuts (1 pound) and Sweetcorn (1 pound).

Cauliflower Cheese (2 pounds cauliflower and when blended add 1 1/2 cups finely grated strong cheddar cheese when reheating.

Crab and Sweetcorn (1 pound of each) and use MILK instead of chicken stock.

Curried Apple (using 2 pounds apples with curry according to taste).

Pea, Lemon and Mint (2 pounds peas with 2 lemons quartered and a generous handful of fresh mint along with stalks.

LUCY WAVERMAN'S TOMATO-ORANGE SOUP

Serves 8

2 pounds tomatoes, peeled, quartered and seeded

1 onion, sliced

1 carrot, sliced

¼ lemon

1 bay leaf

6 peppercorns

4 cups chicken stock

dash salt and pepper to taste

3 tablespoons butter

3 tablespoons flour

2 tablespoons frozen orange juice concentrate

rind of one orange, grated

½ cup light cream

2 tablespoons tomato paste

In a large saucepan, combine tomatoes, sliced onion, carrot, lemon, bay leaf, peppercorns, stock, salt and pepper. Cover and simmer 30 minutes. Blend in a food processor.

In a large saucepan melt butter. Add flour, mix slowly. Add stock and bring to a boil, stirring constantly. Add orange juice, rind, cream and tomato paste. Stir well and heat through.

If served cold, add extra cup of cream and 2 teaspoons of tarragon.

ZUCCHINI SOUP

Serves 4 to 6

1 tablespoon olive oil

1 pound young zucchini, thinly sliced (sprinkle lightly with salt and leave for an hour or so)

½ head lettuce, shredded

6 large green onions, finely chopped

¾ pint chicken stock

freshly ground black pepper to taste

1 bunch chives, snipped

Heat oil in heavy saucepan. Stir in zucchini, lettuce and onions. Stir thoroughly (add a little salt if needed after tasting)

Place lid on saucepan and sauté vegetables gently for approximately 20 minutes. Add chicken stock and freshly ground pepper. Stir.

Replace lid and simmer for 15 more minutes, until zucchini is tender. Whirl in blender.

Serve hot or cold, sprinkled with snipped chives.

PUMPKIN SOUP

Serves 4

1 medium-sized pumpkin

salt and pepper to taste

grated Gruyère cheese, or processed Swiss cheese, (about 1 pound)

stale bread, cut in cubes, sautéed in butter, or toasted in oven (I prefer latter)

1½ cups 35% cream (or so) (I prefer whole milk and a little cream)

Select a pumpkin with a stem. (Be sure pumpkin will hold at least 4 to 5 cups liquid) Cut lid off, clean out seeds and strings. Layer croutons alternately with cheese until it is one third filled. Pour in enough milk or cream to fill the pumpkin ¾ full. Add salt and pepper to taste. Place the lid firmly back on the pumpkin. Place in pan.

Bake pumpkin in 325° F oven for 2 to 3 hours, until outside of pumpkin turns bronze and flesh inside softens a bit — cooking time varies with size of pumpkin. Ladle soup from pumpkin.

Serve in bowls scraping off some pumpkin with each serving.

BON APPÉTIT

BOBBY ORR'S OLD FASHIONED VEGETABLE SOUP

Serves 8

2 to 3 pounds beef bones

1-19 ounce can of tomatoes or 1-10 ounce can condensed tomato soup

1 large onion, diced

4 quarts water

Place all of the above ingredients in a soup kettle. Cover and simmer for 4 hours. Then dice and add:

3 carrots

1 parsnip

1 potato

1 piece of cabbage (about $\frac{1}{3}$ of a head)

$\frac{1}{3}$ medium yellow turnip

2 to 3 stalks of celery

$\frac{1}{3}$ cup of sugar

1 tablespoon salt

(Note: The flavour is its best if you use a meat grinder or food processor for dicing the vegetables.) After vegetables, sugar and salt are added, cook at least 1 hour more.

Remove bones and excess fat before eating. To remove fat, place kettle in refrigerator and chill. Fat will rise to the surface and is easily skimmed away.

MILLER HOWE TOMATO, APPLE, AND CELERY SOUP

Serves 8

½ cup butter

2 cups onions, finely chopped

2½ cups each of tomatoes, apples and fresh celery

½ cup sherry

salt to taste

freshly ground black pepper to taste

3¾ cups good chicken stock

a little heavy cream, whipped

In a heavy-based saucepan, melt the butter and sauté finely chopped onions until golden. Add the tomatoes (if small do not remove the stalk but just wipe clean as there is a lot of flavour in the item and add stalk!), wipe the apples, quarter; wash the celery and add it roughly chopped. Add the sherry along with the salt and freshly ground pepper.

Cover and simmer for about an hour, stirring from time to time to make sure nothing is being caught in the bottom of the pan! Add the chicken stock.

Whirl in blender and pass through a sieve (there is nothing worse than guests finding themselves with a lot of stringy celery in their mouths so do take time and patience with this part of the recipe).

WHEN NEEDED gently reheat (takes about 20 minutes over a low heat).

CHECK SEASONINGS and serve garnished with apple slices and a dollop of heavy cream.

Fresh chives add flavour to this soup or if not available freshly chopped parsley.

HORSERADISH JELLY MOULD *Serves 8 to 10*

1-3 ounce package lemon jelly powder

1 1/2 cups boiling water

1/2 cup mayonnaise

4 tablespoons horseradish

1/2 teaspoon paprika

Prepare jelly powder with boiling water according to package directions. Chill until it reaches consistency of heavy syrup, stirring often (every 1/2 hour).
Fold in remaining ingredients. Pour into mould and chill until firm.
Serve with cold roast beef, perfect for a buffet supper.

MANDARIN ORANGE AND ALMOND SALAD *Serves 6 to 8*

Dressing:

1/2 teaspoon salt

dash of pepper

2 tablespoons sugar

1/4 cup wine vinegar

1/2 cup salad oil

dash of Tabasco

pinch of parsley

Mix well all the above ingredients. Chill.

Salad:

Mixed greens: torn romaine lettuce, head lettuce, spinach, etc.

1 tin Mandarin oranges, drained

Garnish:

1/4 cup slivered almonds

4 teaspoons sugar

Cook almonds and sugar over low heat until sugar is melted and nuts are candied.
Five minutes before serving shake greens and orange sections with desired amount of dressing in a plastic bag. Pour into salad bowl and garnish with candied almonds.

CRANBERRY MOULD

Serves 6 to 8

1-3 ounce package raspberry jelly powder

1-3 ounce package lemon jelly powder

1 1/2 cups boiling water

1-10 ounce package frozen raspberries, thawed

1 cup cranberry sauce, canned or fresh

1-7 ounce can lemon/lime soda pop

Dissolve jelly powders in boiling water.

Stir in thawed raspberries and cranberry sauce. Chill until cold but not set. Carefully stir in soda pop. Chill again until partially set. Pour into a decorative mould, then chill until firm.

Beautiful for a ladies' luncheon table!

MELON POLKA DOT MOULD

Serves 8 to 10

2-3 ounce packages cherry Jello

2 cups boiling water

1 3/4 cups cold water

3 tablespoons lemon juice

8 ounces cream cheese, softened

1 1/2 cups cantaloupe balls

2/3 cup pecan halves

1/2 cup sliced stuffed green olives

mint leaves for garnish

Dissolve Jello in boiling water. Stir in cold water and lemon juice. Pour 1 cup gelatine mixture into 6 cup ring mould. Chill until partially set. Shape cream cheese into approximately 30 small balls. Add one half of cheese balls and one half of melon balls to mould. Around the outer edge of mould, place one half pecan halves. Chill until firm.

Meanwhile chill remaining gelatine until partially set and add remaining cheese and melon balls, pecan halves and olive slices. Pour over first mixture and chill until firm.

Unmould and garnish with mint leaves.

SPINACH SALAD

Serves 6 to 8

Dressing:

1 pint sour cream

2 tablespoons fresh lemon juice

1 teaspoon hot mustard

Combine all dressing ingredients and mix well.

Salad:

2-1 pound bags fresh spinach

½ pound bacon, fried crisply

¼ cup chopped parsley

pepper and salt to taste

Wash and dry spinach. Tear into bite-sized pieces. Toss spinach and dressing together. Place salad in individual salad bowls on a lettuce leaf. Sprinkle with finely chopped crisp bacon and top with chopped parsley. Season to taste.

CAESAR SALAD

Serves 8

½ cup olive oil

2 garlic cloves, crushed

2 heads romaine lettuce, dried and torn into bite-sized pieces

1 egg

3 tablespoons fresh lemon juice

2 teaspoons Worcestershire sauce

1-2 ounce can anchovy fillets, chopped

½ teaspoon salt

¼ teaspoon freshly ground pepper

½ cup Parmesan cheese

2 cups packaged garlic croutons

Combine oil and garlic and let stand overnight. In a large salad bowl, toss greens with oil mixture. Add egg to greens and toss until well coated. In a small bowl, stir lemon juice, Worcestershire, anchovies, salt and pepper. Add to greens and toss again. Sprinkle on cheese and croutons and toss lightly again. Serve immediately.

CUCUMBER CREAM SALAD

Serves 6

1-3 ounce package lime Jello

1 teaspoon salt

1 cup boiling water

2 tablespoons vinegar

1 teaspoon onion juice

½ cup mayonnaise

1 cup sour cream

2 cups finely chopped cucumber, well drained

cucumber curls for garnish

Dissolve Jello and salt in boiling water. Add vinegar and onion juice. Chill until slightly thickened. Fold in mayonnaise. Blend thoroughly. Whip sour cream until light and fluffy, about 5 minutes. Fold into Jello mixture. Fold in cucumber and mix well. Pour into a crystal bowl. Chill until firm. Garnish with cucumber curls.

TOMATO-CHEESE SALAD MOULD

Serves 6

1-10 ounce can condensed tomato soup

2 tablespoons gelatine, soaked in ½ cup cold water and dissolved over hot water

1½ cups chopped celery

1 small onion, chopped

1 green pepper, chopped

1 teaspoon Worcestershire sauce

1 pound cottage cheese

1 cup mayonnaise

Heat soup in a saucepan. Add dissolved gelatine. Stir in vegetables and Worcestershire sauce. In a separate bowl blend cottage cheese and mayonnaise. Add to soup and vegetable mixture. Pour into a decorative mould. Chill until firm.

COLD RICE SALAD

Serves 8 to 10

4 slices bacon

3 cups cold cooked rice

1/2 cup cooked peas

1/2 cup cooked corn

1/3 cup sultana raisins

1/4 cup diced green pepper

1/4 cup diced sweet red pepper

salt and pepper to taste

1/3 cup olive oil

Cook bacon until crisp; drain and crumble. Combine all ingredients except olive oil in a bowl. Toss the mixture with olive oil and chill the salad for at least 12 hours.

A 'must' for a summer picnic.

WATER CHESTNUT LAYERED SALAD

Serves 6

1 medium head of lettuce, torn into bite-sized pieces

3 stalks celery, thinly sliced

1 medium onion, sliced in thin rings

1-10 ounce can water chestnuts, thinly sliced

1-10 ounce package frozen peas

2 cups mayonnaise (or 1 cup mayonnaise and 1 cup sour cream)

3 tablespoons sugar

Parmesan cheese, grated

3 tomatoes

4 hard-cooked eggs

1/2 pound bacon, crisply fried and crumbled

In a deep bowl (preferably glass) arrange in layers in the following order: Lettuce, celery, onion, water chestnuts and lastly, frozen peas. Over this spread mayonnaise (or mayonnaise and sour cream) right to the side of the bowl, sealing the edges. Sprinkle with sugar, then Parmesan cheese. Cover tightly and refrigerate for 24 hours.

Just before serving, decorate with tomatoes and eggs, cut in wedges. Sprinkle with bacon bits.

A very attractive salad.

LIME CHEESE SALAD

Serves 8 to 10

2 cups mayonnaise

3-4 ounce packages cream cheese, softened

2-3 ounce packages lime Jello

1 1/2 cups boiling water

2 teaspoons lemon juice

2 medium cucumbers or 1 English cucumber, finely chopped

1 small onion, finely chopped

1 cup blanched almonds, finely chopped

Beat the cream cheese and mayonnaise together until smooth. Dissolve Jello with boiling water. Add lemon juice. Mix well into cheese and then stir in remaining ingredients. Pour into a large mould and refrigerate until firm.

Make the entire recipe when entertaining and have it for later family dining.

WALDORF SALAD

Serves 6 to 8

3 apples, cored and diced

3 pears, cored and diced

3/4 cup seedless grapes, halved

1/2 cup diced celery

1/2 cup coarsely chopped walnuts

1/4 cup chopped dates

3/4 cup plain yogourt

1 tablespoon powdered sugar

lettuce cups

paprika for garnish

In a large bowl, toss apples, pears, grapes, celery, walnuts and dates. Mix yogourt and powdered sugar together. Pour over salad and toss lightly.

Serve in lettuce cups. Sprinkle with paprika.

BULGARIAN FRUIT SALAD

Serves 6 to 8

3 apples, peeled and thinly sliced

3 pears, peeled and thinly sliced

2 oranges, peeled and sectioned

1 cup pitted sweet cherries and juice

1 cup melon balls

½ cup sugar

2 cups rosé wine

½ cup brandy, optional

Combine all the fruits and sprinkle with sugar. Mix wine and brandy together. Pour over fruit and sugar and mix thoroughly.

Chill for at least 3 hours.

MOJAVE SALAD

Serves 6

Dressing:

½ cup olive oil

½ cup tarragon vinegar

1 teaspoon grated orange peel

¼ to ½ cup orange juice

1 teaspoon sweet basil

1 teaspoon cracked black pepper

½ teaspoon salt

Salad:

1 head cauliflower, broken into flowerets (boiled until tender crisp)

4 or 5 green onions, sliced

½ cup pitted ripe olives

1 head romaine lettuce

alfalfa sprouts

1 orange, peeled and sectioned

Place dressing ingredients in container and shake well. Marinate cauliflower, green onions and olives in dressing. Toss with salad greens and orange sections just before serving.

SALAD DRESSING

Makes 3 Cups

1 3/4 cups oil

3/4 cup malt vinegar

1 1/2 teaspoons salt

1 teaspoon dry mustard

3 tablespoons sugar

1-10 ounce can condensed cream of tomato soup

1 small onion, minced

1 teaspoon Worcestershire sauce (H.P. or A-1)

1 garlic clove (leave in overnight, then remove)

Combine salt, mustard and sugar. Mix and beat in oil, alternately with malt vinegar. Beat until fairly thick.

Add soup, onion and Worcestershire; mix well. Add garlic (leave in overnight; then remove).

PACIFIC LIME MOULD

Serves 20

3-3 ounce packages lime Jello

1-30 ounce can crushed pineapple

3 cups boiling water

3 cups cottage cheese (creamed style)

1 tablespoon horseradish

6 tablespoons mayonnaise

1 1/2 cups whipping cream, whipped

3/4 cup chopped walnuts

Dissolve Jello in boiling water. Drain pineapple and add juice to Jello. Chill until consistency of egg white, then beat until frothy. Fold in remaining ingredients. Pour into a large crystal bowl and sprinkle with nutmeg. Chill at least 12 hours. Can be made 48 hours ahead.

MOE KOFFMAN'S BAVARIAN POTATO SALAD

Serves 6 to 8

8 medium-sized potatoes

3 tablespoons red wine vinegar

1 medium-sized onion, chopped

2 hard cooked eggs, chopped

1 apple, peeled, cored and chopped

3 medium-sized kosher dill pickles, chopped

$\frac{1}{4}$ pound salami, chopped into squares (kosher preferred)

3 tablespoons mayonnaise

salt, pepper, paprika to taste

Peel and boil potatoes. When cooked, drain thoroughly making sure potatoes are quite dry. (A good way to get rid of excess water is to return potatoes to hot element after pouring off water, being careful not to burn.)

Chop potatoes into a large bowl. Add vinegar, onion, eggs, apple and pickles. Fry the salami, lightly and drain off excess fat; cool. Into potato mixture fold in salami, mayonnaise and seasonings. Refrigerate.

This can be kept in the refrigerator for a week to complement any meal.

SOUR CREAM DRESSING

Makes 2 Cups

1 cup sugar

1 tablespoon flour

1 tablespoon salt

1 tablespoon dry mustard

2 eggs

½ cup sour cream

1 cup vinegar

Mix first four ingredients. Add unbeaten eggs, sour cream and vinegar. Beat well. Cook in a double boiler until thickened.

Very good with sliced sun-ripened tomatoes.

SOUR CREAM CHICKEN MOUSSE

Serves 8

2 envelopes unflavoured gelatine

2 cups boiling water or chicken broth

4 chicken bouillon cubes

3 tablespoons lemon juice

1 teaspoon dry mustard

2½ teaspoons curry powder

1 teaspoon onion salt

2 cups dairy sour cream

3 cups or more diced, cooked chicken

1 cup chopped celery

¼ cup chopped green pepper

¾ cup chopped pimiento

¼ cup roasted diced almonds

In a large bowl, sprinkle gelatine over surface of ½ cup of cold water; let stand about 15 minutes to soften gelatine.

Pour boiling water, or broth, over bouillon cubes to dissolve; add lemon juice, mustard, curry powder and onion salt. Pour bouillon mixture over gelatine, stirring until gelatine is dissolved. Let cool about 5 minutes. Stir in sour cream, mixing well, refrigerate until consistency of unbeaten egg white, 40 to 45 minutes.

Fold chicken, celery, green pepper, pimiento and almonds into gelatine mixture; mix well and turn into 1½ quart mould or 8-six ounce custard cups. Cover and refrigerate until mousse is firm.

FOUR ACES DELICATESSEN LASAGNE VERDE

Serves 6 to 8

½ pound lasagne verde

¼ pound Parmesan cheese, grated

½ pound Gruyére or Mozzarella cheese, grated

Cream sauce (Béchamel)

6 tablespoons margarine

6 tablespoons flour

2 cups milk

1 cup heavy cream

salt, pepper, nutmeg to taste

Meat and tomato sauce

¼ pound smoked ham, coarsely chopped

1 cup coarsely chopped onion

2 cups coarsely chopped carrots

½ cup coarsely chopped celery

2 tablespoons olive oil

1½ pound ground beef

2 beef bouillon cubes

2 tablespoons tomato paste

salt and pepper to taste

1-28 ounce can whole tomatoes

2 tablespoons sugar

1 teaspoon garlic powder

2 teaspoons Italian mixed spices

Cook lasagne in boiling water until tender, 15 to 20 minutes. Drain, rinse in cold water and place on tea towel to dry.

Cream sauce: In a sauce pan, melt butter, blend in flour. Add milk slowly, stirring constantly until thickened. Add cream, mix well, add seasonings.

Meat and tomato sauce: In a large heavy saucepan, sauté ham, onion, carrots, celery, oil, beef, until onion is tender and beef is browned. Add all remaining ingredients and bring to a boil. Simmer uncovered for 1½ to 2 hours (to evaporate the excess of liquid).

In an oven proof dish, place a layer of lasagne; then spread a layer of meat sauce; coat with a layer of Béchamel sauce, sprinkle with grated Gruyére. Repeat. Finish by covering last layer of pasta with a generous coating of Béchamel on top of meat sauce. Sprinkle with grated Parmesan cheese. Bake at 375°F for 30 minutes.

BEEF CÉLÈNE

Serves 6

Marinade:

1 cup cooking oil

1½ tablespoons Worcestershire sauce

1½ tablespoons parsley flakes

1 teaspoon black pepper

¼ cup soya sauce

¾ cup dry red wine

2 tablespoons lemon juice

¾ teaspoons salt

Meat:

1-3 pound eye of the round roast

1 cup shrimp

1 tablespoon butter

1½ teaspoon lemon juice

Sauce:

½ cup finely chopped onions

½ cup finely chopped fresh mushrooms

¼ cup butter

dash garlic salt

½ cup dry red wine

Twenty-four hours before serving, mix marinade. Split beef in half lengthwise within one half inch of bottom. Cover with marinade in a small roasting pan. Marinate 24 hours. Remove from marinade, drain for five minutes.

In a small frying pan, sauté shrimp in butter and lemon juice for one minute. Place this mixture in pocket of roast. Close and tie securely with string. Place meat on a trivet in roasting pan. Bake at 425°F for 45 minutes.

Simmer all sauce ingredients, except wine. When onion is tender, add wine. Heat thoroughly and pour into a sauce boat.

FLANK STEAK

Serves 4

2½ to 3½ pounds flank steak

4 tablespoons butter

1 package dried onion soup mix

2 cups water

½ teaspoon ginger

3 tablespoons soya sauce

4 teaspoons cornstarch

2 tablespoons sherry

2 green peppers, sliced

Cut steak into three equal pieces, crosswise. Cut each piece lengthwise along grain into ⅛ inch strips. Melt butter and sauté meat on all sides until brown. Add onion soup mix, water, ginger and soya sauce. Stir. Cover and simmer for 20 minutes. Mix cornstarch and sherry, making a paste. Add to meat mixture. Cook, stirring for 2 minutes. Just before serving, add green peppers. Heat through.

Serve with noodles or rice.

SPAGHETTI CASSEROLE

Serves 4

7 ounces spaghetti

1 teaspoon butter

1½ pounds ground beef

2-8 ounce cans tomato sauce

salt and pepper to taste

1½ pounds cottage cheese

1-8 ounce package cream cheese

¼ cup sour cream

⅓ cup scallions, sliced

1 tablespoon green pepper, minced

2 tablespoons melted butter

Cook spaghetti. Drain. Sauté beef in 1 teaspoon butter. Add tomato sauce, salt and pepper. Remove from heat. Combine cottage cheese, cream cheese, sour cream, scallions and green peppers.

In a casserole, spread ½ spaghetti and cover with cheese sauce; cover with remainder of spaghetti. Pour melted butter on top. Spread tomato meat sauce over top. Bake at 350°F for 45 minutes, or until bubbly.

Serve with green salad and French bread.

BEEF GOULASH, HUNTER STYLE WITH NOODLES

Serves 6

2 pounds cubed stewing beef

4 tablespoons oil

1 cup thinly sliced onions

1 cup thinly sliced celery

1 cup green peppers, cut in strips

1 clove garlic, crushed

3 tablespoons paprika

1 1/2 teaspoons salt

1/2 teaspoon pepper

1 bay leaf

2 tablespoons tomato paste

1-10 ounce can undiluted bouillon

1 cup thinly sliced carrots

1/2 cup sour cream

In a deep skillet or a Dutch oven, with a lid, brown stewing beef in oil. Remove the meat. In the pan juices, sauté onion, celery, green pepper and garlic for approximately 3 minutes. Stir in paprika, salt, pepper, bay leaf, tomato paste, bouillon and carrots. Return meat to skillet; bring to a boil; reduce the heat and simmer, covered, 1 1/2 to 2 hours or until the meat is tender.

You can do this recipe ahead and freeze it, but just before serving time, heat it through, keeping the heat low and stirring in sour cream.

Serve with buttered noodles and a tossed salad.

This excellent recipe is especially good when made with *Moose meat.*

PIERRE BERTON'S CORNED BEEF HASH

Every once in a while, usually on Sunday morning, seized by an urge I can no longer control, I make myself a mess of corned beef hash for breakfast. Nobody can complain that this is a complicated dish. It is simpler to make than a good cup of coffee. If I start at 8:15, I have it on the table by 8:30, the outside crusty and fragrant with an egg sizzling on top of it, and the inside redolent of wine and onions.

I share with you now, a plebeian dish on the face of it, simple to prepare, yet a noble repast.

For if there was ever an all-round, all-purpose meal, then this is it.

It is the perfect breakfast dish, bringing your blood sugar to such a peak that you move through the day as if propelled by some mysterious and hidden energy.

A plate of it made on a Saturday noon hour, when your spouse is away shopping, will bring you to the point where you at last feel able to put on those storm windows — or perhaps take them down again.

But it is equally good late at night, when the television begins to pall and the stomach telephones a small protest to the palate just before bedtime. What better, I ask you, than a plate of this fragrant, sizzling hash to give you wide-screen dreams in beautiful Technicolor, starring long-tressed maidens, gossamer-clad, dancing wildly to moon-mad music?

Its components are proletarian: the lowly potato, the humble onion, and that same bully beef which is said to have won the first Great War for our side — the Spam of its era, the subject of a thousand wry jokes, and Bairnsfather cartoons and some nostalgic memories and old tales told by the fireside.

Why corned beef hash cannot be made of fresh corned beef, I cannot tell, but it is a fact that in this instance, the tinned stuff is far better.

So open a tin of it and crumble the contents into a large bowl. Break it up well into small pieces. I would suggest that you marinate the meat overnight in red wine, but alas, the desire for corned beef hash comes upon you so suddenly that it is almost fashioned in the white heat of passion. There is no time for fancy furbelows, so we must eschew the marination.

When I make corned beef hash I am literally trembling with anticipation. No power on earth could make me wait longer than fifteen or twenty minutes for the first piping hot mouthful. This is why, probably, I always make more of it than I can possibly eat.

So you chop up a large potato and a large onion, dicing them into tiny, tiny pieces. Do not allow any large chunks to slip past the knife. These pieces must be small enough to hold together in a firm mass when they are fried. Not only that but there must be enough outer surface so that there will be plenty of crispness when they are cooked.

Only careful and loving chopping will produce this effect, an attention to detail that is amply repaid also in the case of hash brown and Lyonnaise potatoes, one of which is almost mandatory with steak or ham and eggs.

Now turn the hash over. If it crumbles on turning don't worry; you can easily work it into shape again. Put a second coating of mustard on the top, which should now be crisp and brown with the wonderful odour of the frying hash driving you mad with desire.

Try to control yourself, because there are a couple of necessary rites still to be performed. First, turn the hash over once more so that the mustard is cooked into the corned beef. Then break a raw egg over the whole steaming mass. If the pan is properly hot the egg should cook almost instantly on top of the hash. Stick a fork into the yolk and spread it about a bit so that the whole is congealed into one bubbling unit.

When the white of the egg has thickened and turned milky, take about a tablespoonful of the red wine and carefully pour it into the crevices.

Now you must work very swiftly. Leave the hash cooking only for an instant — long enough for the wine to penetrate and partially evaporate, but not long enough to lose the subtlety of its flavour.

Slide the hash at once onto a plate using a pancake lifter.

And there it is. All you need now is some buttered toast, and a big mug of coffee or a glass of that same red wine, or both, and your morning, or your noon, or your night is made.

The tendency is to wolf this hash as if you were a mad beast that has been starving for days out on the cold tundra. Hesitantly, however, I advise restraint. There are delicate flavours here that are meant to be savoured and not swept aside in the first blind moments of insensate passion.

So sit for a moment contemplating the piping hot repast before you, and approach it with humility. Kings may prefer quail stuffed with the breast of grouse, and duchesses may dote on plovers' eggs pickled in Remy-Martin, but I say there is no dish more truly royal than this peasant fare that is so simple and so quick to prepare. And, when you've made it, you will agree.

But we digress: mix the onion and potato with the corned beef, break a raw egg over the result, and mix again. Then add about two tablespoons of red wine — a good dry, Canadian claret or a Chianti.

Season gently with freshly ground black pepper, celery salt, chopped parsley and monosodium glutamate.

Now sift a small amount of pancake flour into the mixture; not too much, just enough to hold it together. Mix again.

Get a good iron skillet really hot, with a small amount of bacon fat or vegetable oil covering the bottom of it. Ladle out the hash into the pan. I ladle it into fairly small patties about the size of pancakes, which can be easily turned with a spatula but if you like, you can fill the whole pan with the hash.

It will cook swiftly, congealing together into a mass and turning crisp and brown on the bottom. While this is going on cover the uncooked top with a thin coating of dry English mustard, which can be patted firmly into the meat.

MOUSSAKA

Serves 12

2 tablespoons olive oil

3 large onions, chopped

1 green pepper, chopped

2 garlic cloves, minced

6 small zucchini, finely chopped

1 unpeeled eggplant, finely chopped

1-12 ounce can tomatoes, drained

2 teaspoons Worcestershire sauce

few dashes hot pepper sauce

salt, pepper and nutmeg to taste

2¼ cups grated Parmesan cheese

2 pounds ground beef

1 onion, chopped

1 clove garlic, minced

1-8 ounce can tomato paste

In 2 tablespoons oil sauté 3 chopped onions, green pepper and 2 minced garlic cloves. Add zucchini and eggplant and cook until soft. Add drained tomatoes, Worcestershire, hot pepper sauce, salt, pepper and nutmeg. Cook these ingredients down until they can't be distinguished from each other. Put aside. Before adding to large casserole, drain off all excess liquid.

Brown 2 pounds ground beef in heavy pan with chopped onion and minced garlic clove for 5 minutes. Add tomato paste, salt, pepper and nutmeg to taste. Simmer 15 minutes.

Cream Sauce:

4 tablespoons butter

4 tablespoons flour

2 cups milk

1 teaspoon Worcestershire sauce

hot pepper sauce to taste

salt and pepper to taste

Melt butter in saucepan; stir in flour; remove from heat. Slowly add 2 cups milk; return to low heat. Cook, stirring until sauce becomes very thick. Season with Worcestershire, hot pepper sauce, salt and pepper to taste.

In 1 large or 2 small casseroles, layer the mixtures as follows: meat mixture, ¾ cup Parmesan cheese, eggplant, zucchini mixture, ¾ cup Parmesan cheese, cream sauce, ¾ cup Parmesan Cheese.

Bake at 350°F for 1 hour or until top is brown and mixture is bubbly.

Freezes well.

MEATBALLS SUPREME

Serves 4 to 6

1 pound lean ground beef

1 beaten egg

1 teaspoon sugar

½ teaspoon allspice

½ teaspoon pepper

1 teaspoon salt

1 slice stale bread

½ cup milk

½ cup chopped onion

3 tablespoons butter

¾ cup chopped onion

2 tablespoons flour

1 tablespoon tomato paste

1 cup undiluted consommé

½ pound mushrooms, chopped, fresh or canned (1-10 ounce can)

½ cup sour cream

1 teaspoon salt

Mix first 6 ingredients together. Break up and soak the bread in the milk and add to meat mixture. Add ½ cup chopped onion; mix well. Form into small meatballs.

Cook slowly in a lightly greased frying pan about 30 minutes until lightly browned and well cooked. Drain. Melt butter in saucepan. Add ¾ cup chopped onion and brown. Remove from heat. Stir in flour, tomato paste and consommé. Return to heat, stirring until thick. Add the mushrooms and simmer for 5 minutes; add sour cream and salt. Pour over meatballs.

BEEF ROULADEN

Sirloin tip, sliced paper thin (2 slices per person)

bacon

dill pickles

Cheddar cheese

2 small onions, finely chopped

3/4 pound finely cut mushrooms

lemon juice

1 cup bread crumbs

1 unbeaten egg

toothpicks

Sauce:

2 tablespoons butter

2 tablespoons flour

1-10 ounce can condensed consommé soup

Have butcher slice sirloin tip paper thin, allowing 2 slices per person. On each slice of meat, put a piece of raw bacon, strip of dill pickle (cut 1 pickle into 4 slices) and 1 slice of Cheddar cheese.

Make stuffing as follows: Sauté onions; add 1/2 pound mushrooms (save a 1/4 pound for sauce) Cook a little longer. Squeeze lemon juice on top. Add bread crumbs and unbeaten egg. Mix to combine. Divide the stuffing among the pieces of meat and roll each slice up; Secure with toothpicks. Brown the rolls and transfer to shallow baking dish.

Sauce: Melt butter; add flour and blend; add consommé, stir. Add 1/4 pound sautéed, sliced mushrooms. Pour sauce over meat rolls. Cover tightly with foil and bake 1 hour in 350°F oven.

GORDIE HOWE'S BEEF STROGANOFF

Serves 4 to 5

1 tablespoon flour

½ teaspoon salt

1 pound beef sirloin, cut in ¼ inch wide strips (stewing beef may be substituted)

2 tablespoons butter

1 cup sliced mushrooms, optional

½ cup chopped onion

1 clove garlic, minced or 2 teaspoons garlic salt

½ teaspoon paprika

1-10 ounce can condensed cream of mushroom soup

2 cups dairy sour cream

Combine flour and salt. Dredge meat in mixture. Heat skillet, add butter. When melted, add meat, flipping meat to brown on all sides.

Add mushrooms, onion and garlic. Cook 3 to 4 minutes or until onion is barely tender. Add paprika and mushroom soup and simmer 30 minutes. Add sour cream and heat through.

Serve on wide noodles, rice or pilaf.

HE SCORES!!

BOEUF EN CROÛTE (BEEF WELLINGTON)

Serves 4 to 6

1 fillet of beef (2½ to 3½ pounds)

brandy, optional

3 tablespoons butter

½ pound mushrooms, finely chopped

1 Spanish onion, finely chopped

1-14 ounce package puff pastry

1 bunch of parsley, finely chopped

2 hard cooked eggs, chopped

salt and freshly ground pepper

1 egg yolk slightly beaten

Trim fillet neatly, removing ends and if desired, brush with brandy. In butter, lightly sauté mushrooms and onions until soft and transparent. Allow to cool. (This may be done ahead of time.) 1 hour before cooking, roll out puff pastry into a thin sheet, to a size which exceeds the dimensions of the fillet.

1 Spread parsley along the centre of the pastry in a 3 inch strip
2 Add chopped egg on top of parsley
3 Cover with onion and mushroom mixture.
4 Sprinkle liberally with salt and freshly ground pepper to taste.
5 Place fillet on top and wrap pastry neatly around it, securing it at the ends.
6 Turn over and place on baking sheet, seam side down.
7 Make 'twig' and 'leaf' designs on top with remaining pastry.
8 Brush pastry with cold water and bake in hot oven 450°F for 12 to 15 minutes, then reduce oven to 375°F.
9 Brush pastry with slightly beaten egg yolk and continue baking until crust is browned, usually another 20 minutes.

Serve with Béarnaise Sauce

2

Beef Wellington
Recipe on page 64

FRANK AUGUSTYN'S BEEF

Serves 6

1 tablespoon butter

1 large onion, diced

2 or 3 pounds round steak

dash of salt and pepper

paprika

1-10 ounce can mushrooms drained or 1 cup fresh mushrooms

2 or 3 tablespoons sour cream

Brown onion in butter in a deep frying pan. Trim fat off round steak. Cut steak into very fine pieces. Add to frying pan with onions and butter. Sprinkle with salt. Cook slowly until meat is not red. Sprinkle with paprika to make meat red again. A little water may be added.

Cook slowly until meat is tender (about 45 minutes). Add mushrooms; boil a few seconds. Just before serving, stir in sour cream.

This dish can be served with steamed rice and salads.

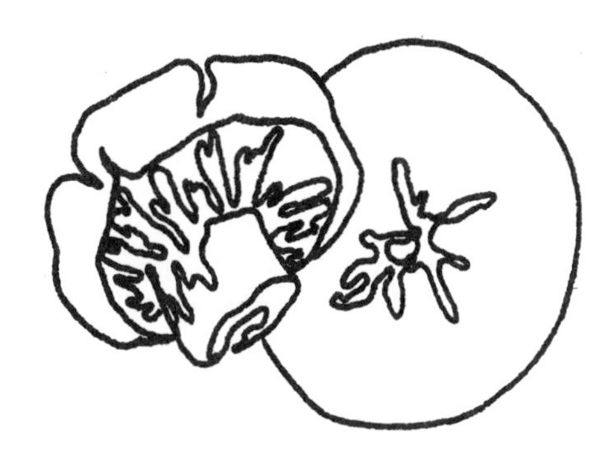

WILD RICE CASSEROLE

Serves 10 to 12

1 cup wild rice

3 cups boiling water

6 tablespoons chopped onion

4 tablespoons oil

1 1/2 pounds ground beef

1-10 ounce can condensed cream of mushroom soup

1-10 ounce can condensed cream of chicken soup

1-10 ounce can condensed consommé

1-10 ounce can sliced mushrooms with liquid

1 cup water

1/2 teaspoon salt

1/2 teaspoon pepper

1/4 teaspoon each celery, salt, onion salt, garlic salt
and paprika

1 tablespoon poultry seasoning

1 bay leaf crumbled

1/2 cup chopped parsley

1/2 cup sliced toasted almonds

Pour boiling water over rice and let stand for 25 minutes. Drain. Meantime, brown onion in oil in skillet until tender; add beef and brown. Mix remaining ingredients except almonds in a large bowl. Combine with drained rice, meat and onion. Turn into a large greased casserole. Bake uncovered at 325°F for 3 hours, sprinkling the almonds over the top near the end of baking. The mixture may be assembled the previous night for baking the next day. Recipe doubles well.

ROBERT GOULET'S CHILI CON CARNE

Serves 8

The following recipe for Chili con Carne must carry the warning that the measurements of the ingredients are approximately correct. It's amazing; sometimes I start out making chili enough for 4 people but by the time I get the correct flavour (too spicy... add another pound of meat; too bland... add more spices, etc) I could probably feed the entire Los Angeles Dodgers baseball team.

Honestly, though, my chili has become quite popular among my friends. They have all dedicated themselves to finding the antidote.

If you like the chili, please drop by the Theatre and let me hear about it. If your feelings run to the negative side, write a nasty letter to Jack Jones.

½ cup butter

2 onions, chopped

6 shallots, chopped

1-7 ounce can green chilies

2 cloves garlic, minced

3 pounds ground sirloin

1 pound sausage meat

2-1 pound cans kidney beans

1-4 ounce can pimiento

3 pounds tomatoes, chopped

¾ cup chopped celery

1 sweet red pepper, chopped

1 hot red pepper, chopped

1-13 ounce bottle of chili sauce

salt to taste

1 tablespoon oregano

4 tablespoons chili powder

1 tablespoon garlic salt

2 tablespoons pepper

2 tablespoons chili sauce

Melt butter in skillet. Add onion, shallots, chilies and garlic. Sauté until soft. Add sirloin and cook until brown. In separate pan, brown sausage. Pour off fat and add meat to onion/beef mixture.

Put meat in large saucepan or dutch oven. Add beans, pimiento, tomatoes, celery, sweet and hot peppers, chili sauce. Bring to a boil; lower heat; cover and simmer 30 minutes. Add salt to taste and rest of spices. Simmer, covered, for 1¾ hours stirring every 15 minutes. Skim off fat.

Before serving add additional chili sauce.

SHIPWRECK CASSEROLE

Serves 15

4 pounds ground round steak, or lean hamburger

2 pounds mushrooms

1 package thin egg noodles

3 Spanish onions

3 green peppers

3 bunches celery

1 large can tomatoes

1-10 ounce can tomato soup

2-10 ounce cans condensed consommé

1 tablespoon soya sauce

3 garlic cloves, crushed

1 cup red wine

½ tablespoon Worcestershire sauce

½ tablespoon oregano

salt and pepper to taste

Day before, brown meat; sauté mushrooms for a few minutes; boil noodles for 10 minutes; chop everything in big bite chunks and add everything together. Stir in wine; let it marinate overnight.

Bake at 325°F for 1½ hours.

GISELLE MACKENZIE'S MY OWN PARTY CHILI

Serves 12

3 pounds ground beef

2 cloves garlic, minced

3 tablespoons butter

2-28 ounce cans tomatoes

3 giant cans kidney beans, drained

4 tablespoons chili powder (more if desired)

several squirts of Worcestershire sauce

seasoned salt and pepper to taste

1 tablespoon fine herbs

1 pound fresh mushrooms, sliced

1-10 ounce can, condensed consommé, undiluted

1 tablespoon dark brown sugar

1 cup chopped onion

Crumble and sauté ground beef and garlic in butter. When brown, add tomatoes and drained kidney beans. Add all the rest of the mess into the pot. Simmer, covered, for 45 minutes to an hour. Taste for seasoning, especially salt, pepper and chili powder. The amount of chili powder should determine whether you want your head blown up or not.

Serve with big hunks of hot French bread with herbed butter and a green salad.

"If you don't like it, go to Mexico."

CORNED BEEF CASSEROLE

Serves 4

1-10 ounce can condensed cream of chicken soup

1 cup milk

1/4 cup minced onion

1-12 ounce can corned beef or ham, diced

8 ounces noodles, cooked

1/2 cup bread crumbs

1/2 cup sharp cheese, grated

Mix chicken soup, milk and minced onion. Place corned beef, noodles and soup misture in buttered casserole. Cover with crumbs.

Bake at 350°F for 30 minutes

BEEF STROGANOFF (FOR A CROWD)

Serves 16

1 cup butter or margarine

1 1/2 cups finely chopped onion

1 1/2 pounds fresh mushrooms, sliced

3 1/2 pounds beef, top round, tenderized, cut in cubes

6 tablespoons flour

3 cups bouillon (or 3 cubes in 3 cups boiling water)

1 1/2 teaspoons salt

6 tablespoons tomato paste

2 tablespoons Worcestershire sauce

3/4 cup sour cream

1 1/2 cups heavy cream

8 cups fluffy cooked rice

Melt 1/3 cup butter in large saucepan and sauté onions until brown. Remove onions and set aside. Melt 1/3 cup butter in same pan and brown mushrooms. Remove mushrooms and set aside. Melt remaining 1/3 cup butter in same saucepan. Roll beef in flour and sauté until very brown. Add bouillon, onions and salt.

Cover and simmer until beef is tender (1 1/2 to 2 hours). Add tomato paste, Worcestershire sauce, sour cream, cream and mushrooms. Heat thoroughly and serve with rice.

Makes 2 large casseroles. Freezes well.

KON KOKI

Serves 8

3 pounds flank steak

6 tablespoons sesame seeds

6 tablespoons salad oil

1/2 cup soya sauce

1 cup finely chopped green onions

2 cloves garlic, crushed

1/2 teaspoon black pepper

1/2 teaspoon ground ginger

4 teaspoons brown sugar

Cut flank steak into serving pieces and score, diagonally, on both sides. Mix remaining ingredients and marinate meat in mixture for 12 hours or overnight. Barbecue steaks, 3 to 4 minutes on each side, while basting with marinade.

BEEF RAGOÛT

Serves 6

2 pounds lean beef, cubed

3 tablespoons fat

2 onions, sliced

6 peppercorns

2 bay leaves, broken

1/4 teaspoon celery seed

1 clove garlic, minced

1/2 cup wine vinegar

1 1/2 cups water

salt to taste

1 tablespoon flour

1/4 cup cold water

Brown beef in fat in heavy skillet. Add onions and brown. Add seasonings, vinegar, 1 1/2 cups water and salt to taste. Stir. Cover and simmer until beef is tender. Blend 1 tablespoon flour with 1/4 cup cold water. Stir into meat mixture. Cook, stirring until thickened.

Serve with sliced tomatoes and hot steamy buns.

AFTERNOON NAP OVEN STEW *Serves 6 to 8*

3 pounds stewing beef, cubed

1 package dry onion soup mix

4 tablespoons quick-cooking tapioca

vegetables: i.e. carrots, onions, beans

1-28 ounce can tomatoes

pinch of salt

salt and pepper to taste

dash of Worcestershire sauce

Place stewing beef in the bottom of a large Dutch oven, or casserole with cover. Sprinkle with dry onion soup and tapioca. Add whatever vegetables you wish. Top with tomatoes, a little sugar, salt and pepper to taste, a dash of Worcestershire sauce, and enough water to cover vegetables. Cook covered for 3½ hours in a 325°F oven. If the stew becomes too thick, add a little water after 3 hours. The longer it cooks, the better it is.

"POT LUCK" PARTY CASSEROLE

Serves 8

6 ounces wide noodles

2 pounds ground beef

2 cups onions, chopped

2 tablespoons butter

1 cup celery, chopped

1-10 ounce can condensed mushroom soup

1-10 ounce can condensed cream of chicken soup

1-10 ounce can mushrooms (and liquid)

1 cup canned water chestnuts, sliced

1 tablespoon Worcestershire sauce

salt and pepper to taste

1 cup Cheddar cheese, grated

Boil noodles according to package directions. Drain, rinse with hot water, drain again.

In a large frying pan,sauté beef with onions in butter. Combine with noodles, celery, soups, mushrooms, and water chestnuts. Season to taste. Turn mixture into greased baking dish and top with grated cheese. Bake at 350°F for 35 minutes until lightly browned.

MAUREEN FORRESTER'S DELUXE MEAT LOAF

Serves 8 to 10

1 package refrigerated crescent rolls

6 ham slices

6 mozzarella cheese slices

2 pounds ground chuck

½ cup dry bread crumbs

½ cup milk

2 eggs, slightly beaten

¼ cup Parmesan cheese

2 tablespoons chopped parsley

¼ teaspoon garlic powder

¼ teaspoon seasoned salt

¼ teaspoon pepper

¼ teaspoon oregano

Mix last 10 ingredients together. Flatten meat mixture to ½ inch thick on waxed paper. Cover with ham, then cheese slices. Roll like a jelly roll. Separate prepared crescent rolls into 4 parts. Wrap pastry (crescent rolls) around meat roll.

Place on a 15 x 7 inch baking dish. Bake at 350°F for 45 minutes.

JANET'S SOUP TO NUTS CASSEROLE

Serves 6

2 large onions, chopped

2 tablespoons butter

1 pound minced beef

½ pound minced pork

4 ounces cream cheese

1-10 ounce can condensed tomato soup

2 tablespoons sugar

½ tablespoon Worcestershire sauce

½ teaspoon salt

¼ teaspoon pepper

1-10 ounce can mushrooms, and liquid

1 cup corn flakes

1 cup unblanched almonds, chopped

½ package noodles

2 tablespoons melted butter

In a large frying pan, sauté onions in butter until tender, but not brown. Stir in beef and pork; brown. Add other ingredients, except corn flakes, nuts and noodles. Simmer for 25 minutes.

Cook noodles until tender; rinse with cold water, drain. Arrange alternate layers of noodles and meat mixture in a buttered casserole dish. Top with corn flakes and nuts, doused in melted butter. Bake at 350°F for 30 minutes.

CASSEROLE OF STUFFED VEAL CHOPS

Serves 6

4 ounces butter

1 small onion

6 large veal chops, 1¼ inches thick

12 mushrooms

2 tablespoons lemon juice

salt, freshly ground pepper

chopped parsley

1 cup chicken stock (or canned broth)

½ cup red wine

1-3 ounce can paté de foie gras

tooth picks or small skewers

Melt butter in a large, heavy skillet. Grate the juice and pulp of the onion into the pan, blend well over moderate heat. Add chops and brown on both sides until very dark. Set aside in an oven-proof dish.

Peel mushroom caps (unwashed), remove stems and slice thinly. In the same skillet (unwashed), add a little butter, lemon juice, salt, pepper and parsley, and sauté the mushrooms and sliced stems over quite high heat for about 4 minutes. Remove the caps to a dish, then add stock to pan and blend with remaining juices and mushroom stems. Add wine and let simmer, over very low heat, while stuffing chops.

Using a small, sharp knife, cut a pocket down the center of the fat end of the cooled veal chop — about ½ inch away from either end and cut right down to the bone. Make the pocket about 2 inches long and fill slit (which will gape open) with about 1 teaspoon of paté a piece. Hold together with tooth picks (or small skewers).

Arrange the chops in the oven-proof dish in which they will be served and pour over them the contents of the skillet. (This much can be done beforehand.)

About 15 minutes before guests are due, place in a 350°F oven to bake for 40 minutes. (This is the minimum time required — can cook 15 to 20 minutes longer.)

STUFFED SWEETBREADS

Serves 4

4 pairs sweetbreads

cold water

boiling water

1 stalk celery

1 bay leaf

1 slice onion

juice of 1 lemon

½ teaspoon salt

⅛ teaspoon pepper

ice water

Soak sweetbreads in cold water to cover for 1 hour. Rinse. Cover with boiling water to which celery, bay leaf, onion, lemon juice, salt and pepper have been added. Cook gently for 20 minutes. Drain and plunge into ice water. When sweetbreads are cold and firm, remove the skin and membranes; cut each sweetbread in half lengthwise.

Dressing:

1 garlic clove, crushed

2 tablespoons butter

1 pound mushrooms, chopped

1 tablespoon flour

1 cup cream

½ teaspoon salt

⅛ teaspoon pepper

¼ cup chopped parsley

Sauté garlic in butter for a few minutes, until tender. Remove garlic and add chopped mushrooms. Simmer for 5 minutes; stir in flour; gradually add cream, salt and pepper, parsley, and cook until thickened. Cool.

Spread the dressing thinly on half the sweetbreads; placing the other halves carefully on top and anchor together with toothpicks.

Place in a buttered shallow casserole dish and spoon remaining dressing around sweetbreads. Pour ½ cup of melted butter over all and bake 30 minutes in 350°F oven. Baste frequently.

VEAL ESPAGNOLE

Serves 4

2 tablespoons butter or margarine

¼ pound mushrooms, sliced

1 large mild onion, thinly sliced

1 green pepper, thinly sliced

1 clove garlic, crushed

2 teaspoons lemon juice

salt and pepper

3 tablespoons olive oil

1 pound veal cutlet, cut in 4 pieces

¼ cup dry vermouth or white wine

2 tablespoons tomato paste

Melt butter in frying pan. Add mushrooms, onion, green pepper, garlic and lemon juice and sauté until vegetables are limp but not starting to brown. Season, then remove vegetables.

In oil in frying pan, sauté veal on both sides until it loses its red color. Season.

Spread half the vegetables in a baking dish which will hold the veal in a single layer. Top with the veal, then with remaining vegetables.

Measure vermouth and tomato paste into the frying pan and stir over heat to remove all browning from the pan. Pour over veal and vegetables and cover. Bake at 325°F for ½ hour. Uncover and bake until veal is tender, about ¾ hour longer. Add a little liquid if needed during baking.

Serve with fluffy rice.

RUSSIAN VEAL

Serves 4 to 6

2 pounds veal cutlets

2 tablespoons flour

1 tablespoon onion juice

2 tablespoons butter

1 cup sour cream

¼ teaspoon salt

1 cup sliced mushrooms

¼ teaspoon paprika

Cut veal in cubes and brown in pan with butter. Remove to a casserole dish, using a slotted spoon. Sauté mushrooms adding more butter, if necessary. Add to casserole with veal. To pan gravy, add flour, seasoning and sour cream. Stir until thickened; pour over meat. Cook in covered dish for 2 hours at 260°F.

The favourite, for the men in my family.

VEAL CORDON BLEU

Serves 6

12 thin slices veal

6 thin slices Swiss cheese

6 thin slices Virginia ham

flour

3 eggs, beaten

¾ cup bread crumbs

¾ cup butter

salt to taste

freshly ground pepper to taste

24 cooked asparagus tips for garnish

Flatten veal slices with a mallet; sprinkle with salt and pepper. Place 1 slice of cheese and 1 slice of ham on each of 6 veal slices; cover with remaining veal slices. Pound edges together with mallet to seal.

Dip each cutlet in flour; then eggs; then bread crumbs. Sauté in butter for approximately 8 minutes.

Season to taste. Garnish with hot asparagus tips.

HONEY AND GARLIC RIBS

Serves 6

6 to 8 pounds back or side ribs

1 teaspoon thyme

2 teaspoons oregano

2 tablespoons garlic powder

2 tablespoons salt

2 tablespoons freshly ground pepper

Sauce:

1 tablespoon garlic powder

1 tablespoon black pepper

1 teaspoon dry mustard

2 tablespoons each Worcestershire sauce, vinegar and soya sauce

½ cup bottled steak sauce

3 tablespoons white wine

½ cup Chinese plum sauce

1-16 ounce jar liquid honey

3 tablespoons molasses

Place ribs in a large pot, cover with water and add next 5 ingredients. Bring to boil and simmer 10 minutes. Remove from heat and allow to cool, covered, for one hour in the liquid.

Meanwhile, mix together the sauce ingredients and blend well. Remove ribs from liquid and place on a broiler pan rack. Brush both sides of ribs with sauce and bake at 400°F until nicely browned, approximately 15 minutes. Serve with remaining sauce.

Marvellous after skiing all day. In fact, marvellous any time.

TOURTIÈRE

There are many different ways of preparing this French Canadian dish. This one is quite light and moist and very flavourful. It also freezes well.

Pastry:
Use your own flaky pastry recipe or, if in a hurry, I have found Robin Hood Flaky Pastry to be excellent.

Using a 10-inch pie plate, prepare bottom crust, place in pie plate and refrigerate.

Ingredients:

3 medium potatoes, mashed

2 tablespoons oil

3 medium onions, chopped

1 garlic clove, minced

3 medium tomatoes, chopped

2 to 2½ pounds lean ground pork

salt to taste

pepper to taste

2 tablespoons ground cloves

1½ teaspoons cinnamon

1½ teaspoons celery salt

2 teaspoons savory

3 tablespoons finely chopped fresh parsley

⅓ cup water

½ cup bread crumbs

1 egg, beaten

Method:

1. Peel, cook and mash potatoes. Set aside.
2. Sweat onions and garlic in oil. Add tomatoes and combine.
3. Add meat to this mixture and simmer until no sign of pink meat remains.
4. Add seasonings and water. (Don't scrimp on salt and pepper). Simmer above until almost dry, 30 to 35 minutes.
5. Add half of bread crumbs to above and let stand for about 10 minutes. If moisture is not absorbed, add rest of bread crumbs.
6. Mix in enough mashed potatoes to hold mixture together. Do not use all of potatoes if not necessary.

Preheat oven to 450°F.

7. Spoon meat mixture into pie shell.
8. Cover with pastry. Crimp edges well and cut slits in top to allow steam to escape.
9. Brush with beaten egg. Bake 10 minutes at 450°F.
10. Reduce heat to 350°F. Cook another 40 minutes.

Serve with homemade chili sauce.

PORK TENDERLOIN EN CROÛTE

Serves 4 to 6

3 large pork tenderloins

4 ounces sliced cooked ham

½ pound puff pastry

1 egg, beaten

Stuffing:

2 tablespoons butter

1 medium-sized onion, chopped

¼ pound mushrooms, sliced

1 teaspoon chopped parsley

1 teaspoon chopped sage

2 to 3 teaspoons bread crumbs

4 ounces ham, chopped

1 egg, beaten

watercress, crabapples for garnish

The day ahead; Split tenderloins and trim, then flatten.

To prepare stuffing: In a frying pan, melt butter and gently cook onions for 2 minutes. Add mushrooms and herbs. Cover; cook for 5 to 7 minutes; remove from heat. Add bread crumbs and ham. Turn into a bowl to cool. Bind with the beaten egg. Divide stuffing in half. Make 2 layers of stuffing between 3 tenderloins. Truss. Bake at 350°F for approximately 1 hour. Baste frequently.

The day of serving: Remove string and wrap tenderloin with 4 ounces of sliced ham. Roll out puff pastry and wrap fillet and ham. Brush with beaten egg. Bake at 350°F for 30 minutes, until well browned.

PORK CHOPS MANDARIN

Serves 4 or 5

4 or 5 pork chops

flour

2 tablespoons butter

1 green pepper, cut in strips

4 or 5 slices pineapple, reserve liquid

3 tablespoons sweet relish

1/2 cup pineapple juice (reserved from slices)

1/2 cup apple juice

1 teaspoon sugar

2 tablespoons soya sauce

1 tablespoon cornstarch

Dip chops in flour and brown in butter. Place in casserole. Sauté strips of green pepper in chop drippings. Put one slice of pineapple on top of each chop, fill centre of slice with a dab of relish and place 2 strips of green peppers on top.

Mix pineapple juice, apple juice, cup water, sugar, soya sauce and cornstarch in pan from chops. Cook until thick and clear. Pour over chops and bake at 350°F for 1 hour.

SWEET AND SOUR SPARERIBS

Serves 4

3 1/2 pounds lean spare ribs

salt and pepper to taste

2 large onions, sliced

1/3 cup brown sugar

1/2 cup vinegar

1 teaspoon soya sauce

2/3 cup pineapple juice

1/3 cup water

1/2 teaspoon salt

1/8 teaspoon pepper

1 tablespoon cornstarch

1 tablespoon water

Preheat broiler. Place spareribs close together on broiler pan and sprinkle with salt and pepper. Broil, turning once, until deep brown on both sides. Place onions in Dutch oven, or large pot, with 2 tablespoons of pork drippings from broiler pan. Sauté onions for 2 minutes. Add next seven ingredients and browned ribs. Cover; simmer over low heat for 2 hours. Remove ribs; thicken sauce with a paste of cornstarch and 1 tablespoon water. Return ribs to sauce. Service while piping hot.

A real family favorite!

ROAST PORK CALYPSO

Serves 6 to 8

1-5 or 6 pound loin of pork

2 cups chicken stock

1 cup brown sugar

2 tablespoons dark rum

2 teaspoons ginger

½ teaspoon cloves

1 bay leaf, crumbled

½ teaspoon salt

¼ teaspoon freshly ground black pepper

¼ cup light rum

2 teaspoons arrowroot (or cornstarch)

1 tablespoon cold water

3 tablespoons strained lime juice

Lightly score the pork by making diagonal cuts ¼ inch deep at 1 inch intervals on the fat side. Place pork scored side up in a shallow roasting pan. Roast at 350°F for 1 hour or until golden brown. Remove loin from pan; skim off fat from juices in pan; pour in stock. Make a paste with brown sugar, dark rum and seasonings. Spread the paste evenly over the scored side of the pork. Return to pan scored side up; roast until done. Transfer loin to a heated platter.

Bring the liquid in roasting pan to a boil. Mix arrowroot and water and add to pan, stirring constantly, until sauce thickens. Remove from heat. Warm the light rum in a small pan over low heat. Remove from heat and ignite. Stir flaming rum, add lime juice. Pour into heated sauceboat and serve with pork.

PORK CHOPS WITH CABBAGE *Serves 4 to 6*

1 large cabbage, shredded

2 tablespoons butter

1 garlic clove, minced

¼ cup onions, finely chopped

salt and pepper to taste

8 pork chops (preferably loin, ¾ inch thick)

3 tablespoons oil and 1 tablespoon butter

½ cup dry white wine

1 cup heavy cream

1 bay leaf

2 tablespoons bread crumbs

3 tablespoons grated Parmesan cheese

2 tablespoons melted butter

Shred cabbage and blanche in boiling water for 5 minutes. Drain well. Sauté garlic and onions in 2 tablespoons butter until soft. Add cabbage and season well. Cook 5 minutes. Transfer to a bowl.

Dry pork chops and season well. Heat oil and butter; sauté chops, approximately 3 minutes each side or until browned. Set aside.

Discard remaining fat from pan and deglaze with wine. Reduce to ¼ cup and mix with cabbage.

Spread ⅓ cabbage on bottom of large casserole; lay 4 chops (singly) on top, ⅓ more cabbage, remaining chops and remaining cabbage.

Heat cream and add to casserole. Place bay leaf on top. Bring to a simmer on top of stove, cover tightly and place in a pre-heated oven, 350°F for 1¼ hours. Remove cover and discard bay leaf.

Mix bread crumbs, cheese and melted butter together, and sprinkle over casserole. Bake at 350°F uncovered for 30 minutes more or until top is brown and crusty.

STUFFED PORK TENDERLOIN

Serves 6

½ cup diced celery
1 medium onion, chopped
1 apple, chopped
2 tablespoons butter
3 cups diced bread
½ teaspoon sage
¼ teaspoon marjoram
½ cup whole cranberry sauce
2 tablespoons brown sugar
¾ teaspoon salt
grated rind of ½ orange
¼ cup fresh orange juice
4 strips pork tenderloin, split
curry powder to taste
oil
1 tablespoon butter
1 cup hot water

Sauté celery, onion and apple in butter. Add diced bread, sage, marjoram and place all in bowl. In a small saucepan mix cranberry sauce, brown sugar, salt, and orange rind. Cook over low heat until sugar is dissolved. Add to bread mixture with ¼ cup orange juice. Stuff pork tenderloin and tie with string. Sprinkle with curry powder and brush with oil. Place in roasting pan on rack. Bake at 350°F for 1 hour.

Baste with mixture of 1 tablespoon butter and hot water.

UPSIDE-DOWN HAM LOAF

Serves 6 to 8

3 tablespoons butter

2 tablespoons corn syrup

1/4 cup lightly packed brown sugar

1/8 teaspoon ground cloves

2 tablespoons prepared mustard

5 slices canned pineapple, well drained

1 1/2 pounds minced raw or cooked ham

1 1/2 cups rolled oats

2 eggs, well beaten

1/2 cup milk

1/8 teaspoon pepper

Preheat oven at 350°F. Melt butter in bottom of loaf pan, brushing the sides. Pour corn syrup, brown sugar, cloves and mustard into the pan; mix with butter. Arrange 3 slices of pineapple on pan bottom. Cut the remaining 2 slices in half and arrange against the sides. Combine minced ham and oats. Stir in eggs, milk and pepper.

Pack into prepared loaf pan. Bake, uncovered, at 325°F for 1 1/4 hours.

Delicious hot or cold.

JAMBALAYA — WITH LEFTOVER HAM

1 large onion, chopped

1 green pepper, chopped

1 clove garlic, minced

1 tablespoon butter or oil

1/2 cup chopped celery

3 fresh tomatoes, peeled and quartered

1 teaspoon thyme

salt and pepper to taste

dash of Tabasco

1/2 cup dry white wine

1 cup rice

2 cups water

2 cups ham, cut into small pieces

Sauté onion, green pepper and garlic in butter or oil, in heavy pan; add celery, tomatoes, thyme, salt, pepper, Tabasco, dry white wine, rice, water and ham.
Put in 2 quart casserole and cover. Place in 325°F oven for 2 hours or until all liquid has been absorbed.
Leftover ham at its best.

GAMMON-IN-A-BLANKET

Serves 4

3 or 4 pounds peameal bacon, in one piece

1 or 2 packages frozen puff pastry

1 egg, beaten

Stuffing:

¾ pounds chestnuts, or 1 can peeled plain chestnuts

½ cup milk

1 onion, peeled and chopped

1 ounce butter

2 ounces bacon, cut in fine slivers

1 tablespoon chopped parsley

3 ounces white bread crumbs

salt and pepper to taste

Simmer peameal bacon in enough water just to cover, for 1½ hours. Cool.
If using fresh chestnuts, cut a cross on each and blanche for 5 minutes in boiling water. Drain and skin.
Simmer skinned (or canned) chestnuts in milk for 30 minutes. Sauté onion in butter over low heat until transparent. Add bacon and sauté until completely cooked. Chop chestnuts and mix with parsley, onion, milk, bread crumbs, salt and pepper. All this may be done ahead of time.

To complete:
Roll out puff pastry; place peameal bacon in centre. Cover with stuffing. Shape pastry around bacon and seal with beaten egg. Place on a well-greased cookie sheet with seam side on bottom. Make 3 or 4 slits on top of pastry and brush entire surface with beaten egg. Bake at 350°F for 45 minutes.
Serve with Cumberland Sauce (a must!).
A less expensive Beef Wellington type dish.

ETTA SAWYER'S ORANGE AND RED CURRANT JELLY TO SERVE WITH LAMB

zest and juice of one orange

1 ½ cups red currant jelly

2 tablespoons vinegar

1 tablespoon chopped fresh mint or 2 tablespoons mint jelly

Cook all together for 5 minutes, strain and chill.

BROILED BUTTERFLY LEG OF LAMB

Serves 6

7 pound leg of lamb

3 cups dry red wine

½ cup olive oil

2 onions, thinly sliced

1 carrot, thinly sliced

1 tablespoon thyme

fresh parsley, bay leaves, garlic cloves

salt and pepper

Have butcher bone and butterfly a 7 pound leg of lamb. Pound it to an even thickness.

In a large glass dish, combine 3 cups dry red wine, ½ cup olive oil, onions, carrot, thyme, 6 parsley stems, 2 bay leaves, crumbled, 2 garlic cloves, crushed and minced, 2 teaspoons salt and ½ teaspoon pepper. Add the lamb and let it marinate, covered and chilled, turning it occasionally for 1 to 2 days. Drain the lamb. Place on broiler rack in pan. Broil the lamb under a preheated broiler 3 inches from the heat for 12 minutes on each side for medium-rare meat. Transfer lamb to a cutting board, let it stand for 10 minutes. cut it diagonally into ¼ inch slices. Arrange on a heated platter.

A beautiful barbecue dish.

ETTA SAWYER'S ROAST LEG OF LAMB IN CRUST *Serves 6*

Have the butcher completely trim and bone the leg of lamb. Spread over the inside surface a mixture made of the following:

2 tablespoons butter

2 cloves garlic, crushed

1 small chopped onion

1 cup chopped mushrooms

squeeze of lemon juice

1 cup coarsely chopped dried apricots (optional)

1 teaspoon dry mustard

1 teaspoon pepper

1 ½ teaspoons salt

Sauté the first six ingredients together for 5 minutes; then add salt, pepper and mustard.

Roll lamb up like a large egg shape, skewer and tie to keep the shape. Place on a rack and bake at 375°F for 1 to 2 hours, depending on size and how well done you like it. When done, allow to cool. When cold, the following mixture is spread over the entire roast before covering with pastry.

1 pound ground pork, or sausage meat

¼ pound liver paté

1 cup chopped mushrooms and ¼ cup chopped onions, sautéed together

salt, pepper and dry mustard to taste

Short Pastry:

3 cups flour (2 cups all-purpose and 1 cup soft wheat flours)

1 ½ teaspoons salt

1 cup butter, lard or shortening or any combination thereof (at room temperature)

Blend together very well with a pastry blender, then finger tips. Mix the following together in a small bowl: 2 eggs plus 2 tablespoons lemon juice. Sprinkle over the flour/butter mixture. Mix well and form into a ball. Cool for ten minutes. Roll pastry out and cover roast. Brush all over with egg yolk, decorate; brush decorative dough pieces also. Bake at 450°F for ten minutes; then at 350°F for 40 to 50 minutes.

With the essence in the roasting pan, make a sauce. Pour off fat; add ½ cup wine and 1 ½ cups Velouté Sauce. Cook for 5 minutes; strain; taste and adjust seasonings.

WORCESTERSHIRE BUTTERED LAMB CHOPS

Serves 4

4 slices side bacon

8 rib or loin lamb chops

3 tablespoons all-purpose flour

½ teaspoon salt

⅛ teaspoon pepper

3 tablespoons soft butter

1 teaspoon chopped parsley

1 teaspoon Worcestershire sauce

pinch of garlic powder

Cook bacon in a large pan until browned; drain on paper towels and keep warm. Dredge chops in a mixture of the flour, salt and pepper and sauté in the bacon fat until golden brown.

Make a Worcestershire butter by combining remaining ingredients. Serve 2 chops per person topped with butter and a slice of bacon.

Bake in 350°F oven for 1 hour. Good with potatoes and broiled tomatoes.

CURRIED LAMB

Serves 6

vegetable oil

2 pounds front of lamb, cut into bite sized pieces

2 large onions, sliced

1 cup carrot, grated

1 cup washed raisins

2 tablespoons curry powder

salt and papper to taste

2 tablespoons chutney

1 cup tomatoes

2 cups water

3 tablespoons flour

In a skillet, brown pieces of lamb in vegetable oil. Transfer to a stewing pot. Place onions, carrots, raisins in the skillet. Stir in curry powder, salt and pepper; brown together, stirring constantly. Add chutney; gradually stir in tomatoes.

Pour this mixture over the lamb, adding 2 cups of water. Thicken with flour. Skim off any excess fat. This lamb dish is all the better if made the day before.

ROAST BONED AND STUFFED LEG OF LAMB

Serves 6

1-6 to 7 pound leg of lamb (boned for stuffing)

¼ cup sliced carrots

¼ cup sliced white turnip

½ cup sliced celery

1 small white leek

1 bouquet garni

1 clove garlic

1 medium sized onion, sliced

1 cup red wine

Stuffing:

½ cup chopped cooked ham

2 ounces ground suet

6 slices day-old bread, crumbled

2 tablespoons chopped onion

1 tablespoon finely chopped green pepper

1 tablespoon finely chopped parsley

1 tablespoon finely chopped celery leaves

3 cooked chicken livers, chopped

1 teaspoon salt

¼ teaspoon pepper

⅛ teaspoon nutmeg

Combine all ingredients for stuffing.

Stuff lamb; sew or skewer together. Place in a shallow roasting pan. Add remaining ingredients.

Roast in a 450°F oven, 25 minutes. Reduce heat to 350°F and roast 2 hours longer. Remove roast from pan. Strain gravy in pan into sauce pan. Thicken with small amount of flour mixed with water.

A gourmet delight.

STUFFED GRAPE LEAVES

Serves 6

1-15 ounce jar grape leaves
1 clove garlic, chopped
4 tablespoons butter
1 onion, chopped
1 1/4 pounds minced lamb, or beef
1 tablespoon lemon juice
1 cup short grain rice, uncooked
2 tablespoons fresh mint, chopped
3 tablespoons fresh parsley, chopped
3 ounces tomato paste
1 cup water
Juice of 1 lemon
1/4 cup vegetable oil.

Drain grape leaves, separate and rinse under cold running water. Blanch in boiling water for 2 minutes. Drain and spread on paper towels shiny side down. Sauté garlic and onion in butter.

In a large bowl blend well minced lamb, 1 tablespoon lemon juice, rice, mint, parsley, tomato paste and onion mixture. Place a small amount of meat mixture on each leaf and roll from stem to tip (like a sausage). Arrange stuffed leaves in layers. Be careful at all times when handling grape leaves as they tear easily. Add water, lemon juice and oil. Cover tightly and cook slowly for 1 1/2 hours. Serve hot or cold.

Poultry

TURKEY AND WILD RICE CASSEROLE

Serves 4 to 6

1 cup wild rice

2 cups cooked turkey

½ pound mushrooms, sliced

1½ cups cream

2½ cups turkey stock

2 tablespoons chopped onion

salt and pepper to taste

½ cup Cheddar cheese, grated

1 tablespoon butter

Wash wild rice in several changes of warm water; soak in cold water for 1 hour. Drain rice; place in a large bowl with cooked turkey, mushrooms, cream, 1½ cups stock, onion, salt and pepper. Turn into a well-buttered casserole and bake, covered, at 350°F for 1 hour. Add remaining turkey stock. Bake 25 minutes more. Sprinkle with cheese, dot with butter and cook 20 minutes longer at 300°F.

GOURMET CHICKEN WRAP-UPS

Serves 4

4 chicken breasts, boned and skinned

1/4 cup butter or margarine

1-8 ounce can refrigerated crescent rolls

1/4 cup deviled ham, canned

milk

sesame seeds

Filling:

2/3 cup finely chopped tart apples

2 tablespoons chopped pignolia nuts or almonds

2 tablespoons raisins, if desired

1 teaspoon instant minced onion

1 teaspoon chopped chives

1/4 to 1/2 teaspoon sweet basil

Sauce:

1-5/8 ounce package chicken gravy mix

1/2 cup cold water

1/2 cup sour cream

Preheat oven at 375°F. Place chicken breasts, boned side up, between 2 pieces of plastic wrap. Starting at centre, pound with a smooth, heavy object until pieces are about 1/4 inch thick. Peel off plastic wrap.

Filling: In a small mixing bowl, combine all ingredients; mix well. Divide filling equally among the 4 breasts. Fold up each so filling is enclosed and fasten with toothpicks. Brown chicken rolls in butter, over medium heat, until golden brown and meat is cooked. (20 to 25 minutes)

Separate crescent dough into 4 rectangles. Press perforations of each to seal; spread with deviled ham. Place 1 chicken roll on each rectangle; fold dough to enclose chicken and seal completely. Place seam-side down on ungreased cookie sheet. Brush with milk; sprinkle with sesame seeds. Bake at 375°F for 12 to 18 minutes until golden brown.

Sauce: In a small saucepan, combine gravy mix and water. Bring to a boil; boil 1 minute. Blend in sour cream. Heat through, but do not boil. Serve hot. Make a lot of this as people like it and use a lot! I double or triple.

Tip: To make ahead, prepare, cover and refrigerate for 2 to 3 hours; bake for 17 to 23 minutes when it has been refrigerated.

W. EARL CAMERON'S CHOP SUEY

Serves 6

2 cups chopped cooked chicken, or pork
2 onions, finely chopped or 3 bunches scallions
2 tablespoons bacon fat
1-8 ounce can sliced mushrooms (1 cup fresh)
2 cups finely chopped celery
salt and pepper to taste
¼ cup water
½ cup cold water
1 tablespoon cornstarch
1 tablespoon soya sauce
1-20 ounce can bean sprouts, drained

Brown meat and onions in bacon fat in a skillet; add mushrooms and brown. Stir in celery, salt and pepper, ¼ cup water; cook until celery is tender and meat cooked.

Mix water, cornstarch and soya sauce; add to skillet. Add bean sprouts; cook for 3 minutes or until heated through.

Serve over steamed rice.

3

W. Earl Cameron's Chop Suey
Recipe on page 96

NANCY C. RAINE'S (NANCY GREENE) OVEN BAKED CHICKEN

Serves 6

8 chicken breasts

1-10 ounce can condensed cream of mushroom soup

3 tablespoons dry onion soup mix

½ cup white wine or chicken broth

paprika or slivered almonds

1 cup sour cream or yogourt

Place chicken, skin side up in baking dish. Mix together soup, onion soup mix and wine. Pour over chicken and bake, uncovered at 350°F for 1 hour. Remove chicken; place on a hot platter, sprinkle with paprika or almonds. Blend sour cream into pan juices; heat gently and serve as gravy. Serve with a mixture of whole grain and wild rice.

BAKED CHICKEN BREASTS SUPREME

Serves 8 to 10

6 whole chicken breasts

2 cups dairy sour cream

¼ cup lemon juice

4 teaspoons Worcestershire sauce

4 teaspoons celery salt

2 teaspoons paprika

4 garlic cloves, minced

4 teaspoons salt

½ teaspoon pepper

1¾ cups dry bread crumbs

½ cup butter

½ cup shortening

Cut chicken breasts in half; pat dry. In a large bowl, combine sour cream, lemon juice, Worcestershire sauce, celery salt, paprika, garlic, salt and pepper. Coat each piece of chicken well with this mixture. Let stand, covered in refrigerator overnight.

Remove chicken from sour cream mixture. Roll in bread crumbs, coating evenly. Arrange in a single layer in a shallow baking dish. Melt butter and shortening in a small saucepan. Spoon half over chicken. Bake uncovered for 45 minutes at 400°F. Spoon over remaining butter and shortening mixture. Bake for 10 to 15 minutes longer or until chicken is tender and browned.

A 'make ahead' gourmet delight!

Excellent served with curried fruit and wild rice.

CHICKEN WINGS IN BARBECUE SAUCE

Serves 6 to 8

24 chicken wings

2 teaspoons salad oil

½ cup diced onion

1 clove garlic, crushed

1 cup diced celery

½ cup diced green pepper

¾ cup water

1 cup smoke-flavoured barbecue sauce or ketchup

2 tablespoons vinegar

2 tablespoons lemon juice

1 tablespoon Worcestershire sauce

2 tablespoons brown sugar

1 teaspoon dry mustard

1 teaspoon salt

¼ teaspoon pepper

Clip off tips of chicken wings. Heat oil in deep 2 quart saucepan and brown wings slowly — a few at a time. Remove chicken; add onion and garlic and sauté until transparent. Return wings to pot. In a separate pan, mix remaining ingredients; bring to boil and pour over wings. Simmer wings, covered, for 10 minutes. Pour into casserole and bake at 350°F for one hour or until tender. Baste occasionally and add more water if necessary. Serve with rice or mashed potatoes.

CHICKEN BREASTS IN SOUR CREAM

Serves 3 to 4

½ pound fresh mushrooms

butter

6 boned chicken breasts

1-10 ounce can condensed cream of mushroom soup

1 cup sour cream

1 cup sherry

Sauté mushrooms in butter. Arrange chickens in casserole dish. In a bowl mix soup, sour cream, sherry and sautéed mushrooms. Pour over chicken and bake at 300°F for 2 hours.

This may seem like a great deal of sauce but it is needed by the time the chicken is cooked, particularly if it is served with rice.

It was recommended to me that I should allow 2 breasts for each man, one per lady!

CHICKEN, ROSEMARY AND ORANGE

Serves 6 to 8

2 frying chickens, cut up

salt and pepper to taste

3 tablespoons cooking oil

2 tablespoons rosemary

garlic powder to taste

paprika to taste

3 cups orange juice

½ cup lemon juice

1½ cups brown sugar

1 or 2 oranges, thinly sliced

Cut up two fryers; salt lightly and fry quickly in cooking oil in a heavy frying pan. Place browned pieces in a large casserole dish. Sprinkle on both sides with salt and pepper, rosemary, garlic powder and paprika. Mix together orange juice, lemon juice and brown sugar. Pour over chicken pieces and cover with orange slices.

Bake in 350°F oven for 45 minutes. Raise heat to 425°F for an additional 15 minutes. Should be beautifully glazed.

BAKED CHICKEN SALAD

Serves 4

2 cups chicken, cut in cubes

2 cups finely sliced celery

½ cup toasted, sliced almonds

1 cup mayonnaise

1 tablespoon fresh lemon juice

2 tablespoons finely chopped onion

2 cups toasted bread cubes

1 - 8 ounce package medium Cheddar cheese, grated

Mix together all ingredients except cheese and bread cubes. Place mixture in a casserole dish; cover with bread cubes; sprinkle with grated cheese. Bake, uncovered at 350°F for 25 to 30 minutes.

The perfect luncheon dish with a crisp salad!

CHICKEN FLORENTINE

Serves 6

4 whole chicken breasts, split and boned

½ cup butter

¾ cup chicken stock

2 tablespoons chopped onion

¼ cup flour

½ teaspoon salt

pepper to taste

nutmeg (dash)

1½ cups milk

½ cup cream

1 egg yolk

1¾ cups grated Parmesan cheese

2-10 ounce packages frozen spinach or 2 packages fresh spinach

Sauté chicken breasts in ¼ cup butter on each side. Add chicken stock; cover and cook 10 minutes or until tender. Set aside. In skillet, sauté onion in ¼ cup butter; add flour, salt, pepper and nutmeg. Slowly add milk and cream; blend well and cook until thickened. Cool sauce. Add egg yolk and ½ cup Parmesan cheese. Cook spinach according to package; drain well, press out all water. In buttered oven-proof dish add layer of spinach, 1 cup Parmesan cheese, layer of chicken. Cover with sauce, top with ¼ cup cheese. Heat in oven at 350°F for 45 minutes.

GARDEN CHICKEN

Serves 4

1 broiler-fryer chicken, quartered (about 2½ pounds)

1½ teaspoons salt

1 teaspoon savory

2 tablespoons butter

1 pound new potatoes, peeled

2 tablespoons snipped chives

2 tablespoons snipped parsley

2 cups chopped celery

1 pound asparagus

1 tablespoon fresh lemon juice

flour to thicken, if you wish

Sprinkle chicken with salt and savory; sauté in butter in a heavy skillet until brown. Add potatoes and chicken to pan and cook, covered for 5 minutes. Remove to 3 quart casserole. Sprinkle chicken and potatoes with parsley and chives. Cover tightly; bake at 375°F for 30 minutes. Add celery and asparagus; sprinkle with lemon juice. Continue baking for 40 minutes more.

CHICKEN MARENGO

Serves 6

1-4 pound chicken, cut into serving pieces

salt and pepper to taste

flour

¼ cup olive or salad oil

1 onion, chopped

½ clove garlic, minced

¼ cup dry white wine

½ cup stewed, or fresh tomatoes, chopped

8 mushroom caps, sliced

Sprinkle chicken with salt, pepper and flour; sauté in oil. Remove chicken and set aside. In pan juices, sauté onion and garlic; add chicken, wine, tomatoes and mushrooms.

Cover tightly and cook slowly until tender, for 40 to 60 minutes. Can be placed in a casserole and cooked in oven at 350°F for 40 minutes.

BONNIE STERN'S CHICKEN BREAST PICCATA

Serves 6

This is a quick, delicious dinner that is very easy to prepare. It is inexpensive yet elegant. It can also be made with veal. Serve with rice or noodles and a brightly-coloured vegetable that is in season.

3 whole chicken breasts, split, skinned and boned (6 pieces or more if required)

salt and pepper to taste

flour for dusting

1/4 cup unsalted butter

3/4 cup dry wine

1/4 cup lemon juice

3 tablespoons capers, well drained (optional)

1/2 cup chopped fresh parsley

2 tablespoons butter

Garnish:

lemon slices

sprigs of fresh parsley

Pat chicken breasts dry, season with salt and pepper and dust lightly with flour. Melt butter in a large heavy skillet. Cook chicken breasts 5 to 8 minutes on each side depending on the thickness of the meat. When chicken is ready, remove to a serving platter and keep warm. A 250°F oven is great for this.

Discard any excess fat in the skillet and return pan to the heat. Add wine and cook, scraping any bits of crust off the bottom of the pan into the sauce. Add lemon juice and cook, over high heat, until the sauce is reduced and slightly thicker. Add capers. Add parsley. Remove pan from the heat and stir in butter. Pour sauce on chicken and garnish with lemon and parsley.

Note: If the chicken breasts are small, buy enough for two per person. Do not overcook the chicken as it is very tender and can become tough easily.

CRUNCHY CHICKEN CASSEROLE

Serves 6

¼ cup butter

3 cups sliced celery

2 teaspoons chopped onion

½ teaspoon salt

pepper to taste

¼ cup all-purpose flour

1¾ cups milk

2 cups sliced cooked chicken

1 cup grated Cheddar cheese

Melt butter in large frypan; sauté celery for 5 minutes; add onion, salt, pepper.
Blend in flour; gradually stir in milk. Cook until thickened. Stir in chicken and cheese. Turn into a greased 6 cup casserole. Sprinkle with topping.

Topping:

½ cup flour

⅛ teaspoon salt

¼ cup butter

½ cup grated Cheddar cheese

½ cup sliced toasted almonds

Combine flour and salt. Cut in butter until mixture resembles meal. Mix in cheese and almonds. Sprinkle over casserole.
Bake at 400°F for 25 minutes.

CHICKEN AND ASPARAGUS CASSEROLE

3 tins asparagus tips drained, or 2 pounds fresh cooked asparagus

12 slices cooked chicken

2-10 ounce cans condensed mushroom soup

1 cup whipping cream

1/4 teaspoon curry powder

4 drops Tabasco sauce

4 tablespoons chopped pimientos

4 tablespoons Parmesan cheese

Layer asparagus in bottom of a 12 inch casserole pan. Place cooked chicken over asparagus. Mix together soup, whipping cream, curry powder, Tabasco sauce and pimientos and cook until smooth. Pour over chicken, sprinkle with Parmesan cheese.

Bake uncovered at 400°F for 20 minutes. Place under broiler until browned (2 minutes). Sprinkle with Parmesan cheese and serve.

CHICKEN AND ALMOND CASSEROLE

Serves 4

4 cups cooked chicken

2/3 cup toasted almonds

4 hard cooked eggs, sliced

3/4 cup mayonnaise

1-10 ounce can condensed cream of chicken soup

2 pimientos, finely chopped

2 teaspoons lemon juice

1 teaspoon salt

1 tablespoon minced onion

1 cup Cheddar cheese, grated

1 1/2 cups potato chips, crushed

Combine all but last 2 ingredients. Place in a greased casserole dish, top with cheese, then chips. Cover and refrigerate overnight. Bake uncovered at 400° F for 25 minutes.

NEVER-FAIL CHICKEN DIVAN

Serves 6

2-10 ounce packages frozen broccoli spears, cooked

4 whole chicken breasts (8 halves), cooked

2-10 ounce cans condensed cream of chicken soup

1 cup mayonnaise

1 teaspoon lemon juice

dash of sherry

½ cup bread crumbs

½ cup grated sharp Cheddar cheese

1 tablespoon butter, melted

Place cooked broccoli on bottom of a 13 x 9 inch baking dish. Cover with cooked chicken pieces. In a bowl, mix soup, mayonnaise, lemon juice and sherry. Pour sauce over chicken. Cook, covered with foil, at 350°F for 30 minutes.

Remove from oven; sprinkle with bread crumbs; cover with cheese; drizzle with melted butter. Return to oven and bake for an additional 10 minutes.

POULET AU VINAIGRE

Serves 4

2 whole chicken breasts (4 large halves)

¼ cup butter

3 shallots, or 1 clove garlic, finely chopped

3 tablespoons red wine vinegar

½ cup consommé

pinch tarragon

pinch pepper

1 large tomato, peeled, seeded and diced

1 tablespoon butter } Sauce
1 tablespoon red wine vinegar }

Brown chicken in a skillet, in butter. Remove chicken, set aside. Drain off all but 1 tablespoon of butter from skillet. Add shallots and sauté until soft. Stir in vinegar, consommé and seasonings. Bring to a boil; add tomato. In a casserole dish, place consommé and chicken breasts. Bake, uncovered at 350°F for 50 minutes. In a small saucepan melt 1 tablespoon butter and stir in 1 tablespoon red wine vinegar. Pour over cooked chicken first before serving.

LIZ PRIMEAU'S BREAST OF CHICKEN WITH STUFFED MUSHROOMS

Serves 4 to 6

6 large chicken breasts, boned and skinned

1/2 cup bread crumbs

1/4 cup wheat germ

1/4 teaspoon thyme (try tarragon or oregano to vary flavour)

oil

butter

3/4 cup Madeira

Mix bread crumbs, wheat germ and seasoning. Firmly press each chicken breast into this mixture to coat both sides. Chill 15 minutes to set crumbs.
Heat butter and oil in frying pan; lightly brown chicken on both sides. Transfer to a shallow casserole in a single layer or overlapping slightly. Add Madeira to pan and boil briskly until reduced by one third, scraping up browned particles; pour over chicken.

Arrange mushrooms alongside chicken in casserole, cover tightly and bake 1/2 hour at 325°F. Do not overcook or chicken will toughen. Serve from casserole at the table.

STUFFED MUSHROOMS

12 large, fresh mushrooms

butter

1 clove garlic, chopped finely

1 medium onion, chopped finely

1/4 cup bread crumbs

1/2 cup spinach, cooked, squeezed dry and chopped

salt, pepper and nutmeg to taste

Wash mushrooms and remove stems. Chop stems finely. Melt butter in frying pan and sauté garlic and onion until transparent. Add mushroom stems and cook one minute. Add spinach and cook until moisture has almost completely disappeared. Remove from heat; add bread crumbs, and seasonings, and mix well. Fill mushroom caps, rounding mixture and pressing it down so that it holds its shape.

Note: Ground veal or pork (1/4 pound) can be substituted for spinach for a change of taste.

DUCKLING IN BLACK CHERRY SAUCE

Serves 4

Roast a well-seasoned duck, don't overcook! Cool and cut into serving pieces. Place pieces in a casserole dish.

Sauce:

2-10 ounce tins black cherries

½ cup brown sugar

½ cup red wine

3 tablespoons cornstarch

water

2 teaspoons lemon juice

In a saucepan boil together black cherries, brown sugar and red wine. Make a paste of cornstarch, water and lemon juice. Stir into cherry-sugar mixture and boil gently until thick and clear.

Pour over duckling in casserole dish and bake at 325°F for 30 minutes; then carefully slip under broiler until bubbling.

Serve at once! Scrumptious!

Seafood

CAFÉ DU MIDI, LONDON, ONTARIO SEAFOOD PILAF

Serves 12 generously

½ pound sweet butter

4 or 5 green onions, chopped

⅛ teaspoon nutmeg

¼ teaspoon basil

⅛ teaspoon thyme

4 large Spanish onions, minced

1 teaspoon salt

¾ teaspoon pepper

1 cup flour

4 cups heavy cream

6 cups fish stock

¼ cup chopped parsley

2 pounds scallops

2 pounds shrimp

2 pounds crab, cooked

2 tablespoons lemon juice

To cook seafood and make stock:

Boil 2 quarts of water with salt, 1 whole lemon and 3 bay leaves. Cook scallops in boiling water for 2½ minutes. Remove. Using same water, cook shrimp for 3½ to 5 minutes (just until they peel easily) and remove. Strain cooking water and use 6 cups for your stock. If you have time, reduce this liquid on high heat until all you have is 6 cups. This gives more flavour to the finished product.

Method:

Melt butter on low heat in a heavy bottomed pot. Add all the ingredients from green onions to pepper. Cook on low heat until onions are soft; do not brown. Add flour and cook stirring now and then for 3 to 5 minutes. Add stock and cream and beat with a wire whisk until well mixed. Cook on medium high heat using wire whisk constantly. Do not let sauce stick to the bottom; it scorches and turns brown very fast. Add cooked seafood, parsley and lemon juice; mix well.

Serve on rice.

CLYDE GILMOUR'S KAGOOLASH (SALMON CURRY CASSEROLE WITH EGGS)

Serves 3 to 4

2 hard-boiled eggs

3/4 cup macaroni (cut)

1 1/2 tablespoons butter

1 1/2 tablespoons flour

1 teaspoon curry powder

pinch each of salt and pepper

1 cup milk

1-7 1/2 ounce can red salmon

1 cup corn flakes

Hard boil eggs; run under cold water, shell and refrigerate. Cook macaroni in salted boiling water until tender. Meanwhile melt butter; add flour, curry, salt and pepper; cook and stir for a few minutes. Add milk: cook and stir until you have a smooth cream sauce.

Preheat oven to 350°F. Open salmon and break into small chunks. Add it, with its liquid, to the sauce. Drain and rinse macaroni, add to the salmon mixture. Mix gently. Put half into a buttered casserole. Slice or quarter eggs and place on top. Add rest of salmon sauce. Crush corn flakes and sprinkle over top. Dot with butter. Cook, uncovered, for approximately 20 minutes.

A tossed green salad; or watercress, tomato and cucumber slices; or a spinach salad with raw mushrooms, goes well with this dish.

SEAFOOD CASSEROLE

Serves 8

1 ½ pounds haddock

1 pound shrimp (optional)

garlic salt

pepper

juice of 1 lime

2 medium potatoes, peeled and sliced

1 large onion, thickly sliced

1 large green pepper, seeded, cut in strips

⅓ cup oil

½ cup tomato sauce

½ cup catsup

½ cup dry white wine

1 tablespoon vinegar

1 teaspoon Worcestershire sauce

1 teaspoon salt

1-4 ounce tin pimientos, chopped

1 cup frozen peas

4 ounces chopped, stuffed olives

Place fish and shrimp in a shallow dish, sprinkle lightly with garlic salt and pepper, cover with lime juice. Refrigerate 1 hour.

Cover the bottom of a heavy Dutch Oven with slices of potato. Place the fish on top of the potato and cover with onion slices and green pepper. Combine oil, tomato sauce, catsup, wine, vinegar, Worcestershire sauce, salt; pour over casserole. Add a few bay leaves, cover tightly and bring to the boil. Reduce heat and simmer 45 minutes. Add pimientos, peas and olives. Simmer an additional 15 minutes.

SEAFOOD CASSEROLE

Serves 6

1 cup raw shrimp

1 cup fresh or canned crab

1 cup scallops

buttered crumbs

Combine seafood in sauce, place in greased baking dish, cover with buttered crumbs and bake at 375°F for 30 minutes.

Sauce:

1 tablespoon butter

4 green onions, cut in 1/2 inch lengths

2 tablespoons flour

2 cups milk (part cream)

dash cayenne

1/2 teaspoon paprika

1/2 teaspoon dry mustard

1/2 garlic clove or 1/2 teaspoon garlic salt

2 cups shredded sharp cheese

2 teaspoons chopped pimientos

1/2 cup sherry

Method:

Melt butter in pan, cook onions for two minutes. Sprinkle in flour. Cook roux gently for two minutes; add milk, seasonings and cook sauce until thickened and smooth. Stir in cheese and pimiento. When cheese has melted, remove from heat. Add sherry.

COQUILLES ST. JACQUES PRINTANIER

Serves 6

Poaching Bouillon:

1 cup white wine

1 cup water

1 carrot, sliced

1 celery stalk, chopped

1 onion, stuck with a clove

bouquet garni (parsley, bayleaf, celery stalk in cheesecloth)

½ teaspoon thyme

6 or 8 pepper corns

2 garlic cloves

½ teaspoon salt

1 ½ pounds scallops, washed

1 ½ cups carrots, sliced or julienne

1 cup peas

1 cup small onions

Sauce:

2 egg yolks

¾ teaspcon dry mustard

2 teaspoons Dijon mustard

1 cup heavy cream

4 tablespoons butter

3 tablespoons flour

juice of lemon

salt and pepper to taste

2 tablespoons butter

¼ to ½ cup bread crumbs

In a saucepan, combine all ingredients for the poaching bouillon; simmer 20 minutes. Add scallops, cover, simmer 5 minutes. Remove scallops to a side dish. Strain bouillon. Reduce bouillon over high heat to 1 ½ cups liquid.

Cook each vegetable separately until just tender, refresh in cold water, put aside. *Sauce:* In a small bowl, combine egg yolks, dry mustard and Dijon mustard. Add heavy cream and whisk until well blended. In a saucepan melt butter; when hot stir in flour; cook for 2 to 3 minutes stirring constantly. Do not brown. Slowly add bouillon, stirring all the time, until mixture thickens. Simmer 8 to 10 minutes, whisking several times. Lower heat, whisking egg/cream mixture. Be sure not to let it boil. Remove from heat; add juice of lemon, salt and pepper to taste; whisk in 2 tablespoons butter. Place seafood and vegetables in casserole. Pour sauce over; cover with bread crumbs. Bake in oven at 350°F for 15 minutes.

A dinner party delight!

COQUILLE ST. JACQUES

Serves 6

1 pound fresh scallops

1 cup white wine

1/4 cup water

1 onion

salt and pepper

bouquet garni (bay leaf, parsley, celery stalk, 6 pepper corns)

1/4 pound mushrooms

juice of 1 lemon

buttered bread crumbs

Wash scallops; simmer slowly in white wine and water, with onion, salt, pepper and bouqet garni for 5 or 6 minutes.

Drain scallops, saving liquid, cut into small neat pieces. Place liquid back on stove; boil and cook down until you have one cup left. Slice mushrooms, combine with lemon juice, cook 4 minutes.

Bechamel Sauce:

3 tablespoons butter

3 tablespoons flour

1 cup milk

1/2 cup scallop liquid

1 egg yolk

Melt butter, stir in flour, cook until smooth and bubbly. Stir in milk and cook slowly, stirring constantly, until mixture thickens. Stir in scallop liquid. Beat egg yolk; pour sauce over egg yolk very slowly, stirring constantly.

Combine scallops, mushrooms and sauce. Fill six scallop shells. Sprinkle with buttered bread crumbs; brown under broiler; serve immediately.

OYSTER CASSEROLE # 1

Serves 6

1 pint oysters, with liquor
1/4 cup butter
1 cup chopped onion
1/4 cup chopped celery
1 cup liquid (oyster liquor and water)
3 large tomatoes, peeled and chopped
1/2 cup white wine
3/4 cup long grain rice
2 teaspoons salt
1/2 teaspoon pepper
dash cayenne
dash nutmeg
1-12 ounce package frozen peas

Preheat oven to 325°F. Generously butter a 3 quart casserole. Drain oysters, reserving liquor. In a skillet, melt butter; add onions and celery and sauté, gently stirring, for 3 minutes. Add 1 cup liquid, tomatoes, wine, rice, salt, pepper, cayenne and nutmeg. Bring to a boil. Remove from heat and add the peas. Pour into the prepared casserole; cover and bake for 1 hour (until rice is tender). Remove from oven and press the oysters deep into the hot rice; return to oven for 10 minutes.

Serve with a green salad.

OYSTER CASSEROLE # 2

Serves 8

6 cups cracker crumbs
2 teaspoons salt
1/2 teaspoon pepper
3 pints of oysters, with liquor
1 1/2 cups butter, softened
1 1/2 pints whipping cream

If oysters are in shells, shell, reserve juice, and cut in half. If in pint jars, halve, and reserve juice. Mix crumbs with butter. Put half the crumbs in the bottom of a casserole dish; cover with all the oysters, and liquor, salt and pepper; then the rest of the crumbs.

Pour the cream over the entire casserole. Bake at 350°F for 20 minutes.

SHRIMP AND WILD RICE CASSEROLE

Serves 4

2 tablespoons chopped green pepper

2 tablespoons chopped onion

2 tablespoons butter

2 cups cooked wild rice

1-10 ounce can condensed cream of mushroom soup

1 tablespoon lemon juice

½ teaspoon dry mustard

½ teaspoon Worcestershire sauce

½ cup cubed Cheddar cheese

½ pound, or more, or shelled, deveined, uncooked shrimp

In a skillet, sauté the onion and green pepper in butter. Add wild rice, mushroom soup, lemon juice, dry mustard, Worcestershire sauce, cheese and shrimp.

Mix and bake in 1½ quart casserole at 375°F for 30 to 40 minutes.

SHRIMP AND MUSHROOM RING

Serves 6

2 tablespoons butter

3 stalks celery, chopped

4 green onions, chopped

½ green pepper, chopped

½ pound fresh mushrooms, sliced

15 fresh shrimp, cooked and cut into thirds

6 slices bacon, crisply cooked and crumbled

parsley

3¾ cups chicken broth

½ cup long grain rice

juice of 1 lemon

salt and pepper to taste

Brown celery, onions, pepper and mushrooms in butter, in a frying pan. Add remaining ingredients; bring to a boil. Cover. Cook at medium heat for 25 to 30 minutes. Pour into ring mould and serve.

TUNA SOUFFLÉ

Serves 4

½ cup mayonnaise

¼ teaspoon garlic salt

⅓ teaspoon pepper

4 tablespoons flour

4 tablespoons milk

1¼ cups flaked tuna

4 egg whites, well beaten

pinch of thyme

Parmesan cheese

Mix together the first ingredients; slowly add milk; then tuna. Fold in beaten egg whites, then thyme. Pour into a well-buttered 2 quart soufflé dish. Sprinkle with Parmesan cheese. Bake at 350°F for 45 minutes.

Easy, and nutritious!

FILLET OF SOLE

Serves 6

4 large fillets of sole (or 8 small)

1 tablespoon onion, mixed

dry white wine

16 shrimps, cooked

16 mushrooms, sliced

2 tablespoons butter

salt, freshly ground pepper to taste

2 teaspoons butter } kneaded together

2 teaspoons flour }

parsley or chives, finely chopped

lemon wedges

Arrange sole in a shallow, buttered baking dish (that has a cover). Sprinkle with onion and barely cover with wine. Scatter shrimp and mushrooms over sole, dot with butter, season lightly with salt and pepper. Cover with buttered parchment, or waxed paper; then the baking dish lid. Bake for 10 minutes in a 350°F oven. Remove long enough to stir in kneaded butter and flour; replace in oven, covered, for an additional 10 minutes. Sprinkle with chives or parsley. Serve with lemon wedges.

OYSTER CHOW MEIN

Serves 4 to 6

2 large stalks celery

1 medium onion

1 medium green pepper

1/4 cup (1/2 stick) margarine or butter

1 pint shucked Maryland oysters, with liquor

2 tablespoons margarine or butter

1-4 ounce can mushrooms

2 tablespoons flour

1-1 pound can bean sprouts, drained

2 tablespoons Teriyaki sauce

Salt and pepper to taste

1-5 1/2 ounce can chow mein noodles

Chop celery, onion and green pepper. Put into 12 inch skillet and sauté in margarine or butter until tender. Remove from heat.

In another pan, cook oysters in 2 tablespoons margarine or butter until edges of oysters just begin to curl. Remove from heat. With slotted spoon, put oysters into skillet with vegetable mixture.

Drain mushrooms, reserving juice. Add enough mushroom juice to oyster liquid to make 3/4 cup. Stir flour into oyster liquid and cook over medium heat, stirring constantly, until mixture comes to a boil and thickens. Gently stir into oyster mixture along with mushrooms, bean sprouts and seasonings. Cook slowly until heated through.

Serve over chow mein noodles.

DEVILLED SEAFOOD

Serves 8

2 pounds haddock fillets

1 pound lobster meat (canned or frozen)

2 tablespoons corn oil

4 tablespoons flour

2½ cups milk

2 tablespoons cornstarch

½ cup sherry

1 tablespoon lemon juice

2 tablespoons horseradish

1 clove garlic, minced

2 teaspoons French mustard

½ teaspoon salt

1 teaspoon soya sauce

4 tablespoons parsley, chopped

1 teaspoon Worcestershire sauce

1 teaspoon corn oil

bread crumbs

Grease inside of top of a double boiler; add fish; cover and cook over boiling water for about 20 minutes.

Separate fillets and lobster meat into bite-sized pieces.

In a saucepan, blend 2 tablespoons oil and flour. Slowly add milk. Cook until bubbly, stirring constantly. Add cornstarch, blended with sherry. Cook ten minutes over medium heat.

Add all remaining ingredients except bread crumbs and oil, including fish and lobster. Pour into an oiled 3 quart casserole. Top with crumbs tossed in oil. Bake 30 minutes uncovered at 400°F.

QUICK AND EASY FRIED OYSTERS

Serves 4

1 to 2 cups dry pancake mix (any type)

1 pint shucked Maryland oysters, drained

Fat or oil for frying

Salt

Cocktail or tartar sauce

Put pancake mix into large shallow bowl. Add oysters, a few at a time and toss lightly until well-coated. Shake off excess breading in wire basket. Fry in deep fat at 350°F until golden brown, 1 1/2 to 2 minutes. Drain on paper towel.

Repeat process until all oysters are cooked. Salt lightly and serve with cocktail or tartar sauce.

NOTE: Equal results can be obtained by frying oysters in 1 to 2 inches hot fat or oil in large fry pan. Keep turning oysters until browned.

SHRIMP STROGANOFF

Serves 4

1/4 cup butter

1/4 cup onion, minced

1 1/2 pounds raw shrimp, shelled and deveined

1/2 pound mushrooms, quartered

1 tablespoon butter

1 tablespoon flour

1 1/2 cups sour cream, room temperature

1 1/4 teaspoon salt

pepper to taste

Saffron rice

artichoke hearts

In a large skillet, sauté onion in butter until tender. Add shrimp and sauté 3 to 5 minutes or until pink and just cooked. Transfer the mixture to a heated dish and keep warm.

To the skillet add mushrooms and butter; sauté until brown. Sprinkle mushrooms with flour and cook the mixture, stirring, for 2 minutes. Reduce heat to low and stir in shrimp mixture; add sour cream, salt and pepper. Cook, stirring, for 2 to 3 minutes, or until the shrimps are heated through. DO NOT BOIL.

Serve the Stroganoff over saffron rice tossed with artichoke hearts.

OLD LINE OYSTER PIE

Serves 6 to 8

pastry for double crust 9 inch pie

2 cups thinly sliced potatoes, slightly undercooked

1 pint oysters with liquor

4 hard-cooked eggs, shelled and sliced

¼ cup butter

celery salt, to taste

lemon pepper seasoning

Place bottom crust in pie pan. Fill with well-drained potatoes. Drain oysters reserving liquor, for sauce. Arrange oysters over potatoes. Place egg slices on top of oysters. Dot butter over the entire pie filling; sprinkle with celery salt and lemon-pepper seasoning. Place top crust on pie and cut slits in the pastry.

Bake at 400°F for 10 minutes; lower heat and bake at 375° F until crust is lightly browned; about 30 minutes. Let stand for a few minutes before serving (drain off any excess liquid) Serve with Oyster Sauce.

Oyster Sauce:

2 tablespoons butter

2 tablespoons flour

1 cup milk

oyster liquor plus water to equal ½ cup

salt and pepper to taste

In a saucepan melt butter, mix in flour. Slowly add milk, then oyster liquor, stirring constantly. Cook, stirring until mixture comes to a boil and thickens. Add salt and pepper. Serve hot with the pie.

CYNTHIA WINE'S SHRIMP CURRY

Serves 4 to 6 liberally

3 cups whole milk

2 cups dried shredded coconut

1/2 cup butter

6 small onions, finely chopped

2 cloves garlic, minced

1/4 teaspoon ground cumin

1/8 teaspoon cayenne pepper

1 teaspoon ground ginger

1 tablespoon good quality curry powder

2 teaspoons salt

2 ripe tomatoes, chopped

2 tablespoons flour

1 medium cucumber, pared and cubed

4 cups pieces of cooked shrimp

2 tablespoons lemon juice

1 tablespoon brown sugar

Combine milk and shredded coconut in a saucepan. Bring to a boil, remove from the heat; let stand 30 minutes. Press all milk from the coconut and discard the pulp.

In a large skillet, with cover, melt butter and sauté onions and garlic about 10 minutes, or until transparent, but not browned, stirring constantly. Blend in a mixture of cumin, cayenne, ginger, curry powder and salt with the tomatoes. Cover and simmer 15 minutes, stirring occasionally. Add flour gradually, stirring constantly. Slowly add the coconut milk, stirring steadily until the boiling point is just reached. DO NOT BOIL! Reduce heat: stir in cucumber and shrimp and simmer 10 minutes, stirring carefully but thoroughly. Mix lemon juice and brown sugar and blend with the mixture. Simmer 5 minutes, correct seasoning if necessary and serve with hot steamed rice.

PEACE MAKER

Serves 4

1 loaf Italian bread

8 slices bacon

¼ pint (8 ounces) shucked Maryland oysters, drained

Flour, for sprinkling

2 medium tomatoes

Salt and pepper to taste

½ cup sour cream

1 teaspoon horseradish

Slice bread lengthwise; scoop out soft bread inside to form a shell.

In skillet, fry bacon until crisp. Remove and drain. Sprinkle oysters with flour and fry in bacon fat until browned on both sides. Remove and keep warm. Slice tomatoes and cook in remaining bacon fat until heated through. Remove from skillet and sprinkle with salt and pepper.

Layer bacon, tomatoes and oysters in the bread shell and wrap in aluminum foil. Bake at 350°F. until heated through, 15 to 20 minutes. Cut diagonally into slices.

Mix sour cream and horseradish and serve as a sauce.

SHRIMP MOUSSE

Serves 4 to 6

1-10 ounce can condensed tomato soup

1-8 ounce package of cream cheese

2 envelopes unflavoured gelatin

½ cup cold water

1 cup mayonnaise

1 cup celery, finely chopped

½ cup green pepper, finely chopped

1½ pounds cooked shrimp

juice of lemon

onion juice, to taste

1 tablespoon Worcestershire sauce

Tabasco

Heat undiluted can of tomato soup and stir in cream cheese. Dissolve gelatin in ½ cup cold water and add to hot soup mixture. Let cool.

Add mayonnaise, celery and green pepper. Chop the shrimp finely and stir into mixture. Season with lemon juice, onion juice, Worchestershire and Tabasco.

Pour into mould and allow to set.

FISH AND BEER BATTER

Enough for 8 or 10 Fillets of Fish

2 tablespoons pancake mix

1 teaspoon salt

1 egg yolk, slightly beaten

2 tablespoons melted butter

½ cup beer

1 egg white, well beaten

Mix together pancake mix, salt, egg yolk, melted butter and beer. Set aside for a short time, (if too watery, add more pancake mix). Just before using, add stiffly beaten egg white.

Dredge fish fillets in flour; then dip in batter; fry in butter.

SWEET AND SOUR SHRIMPS

Serves 8

2 pounds cleaned, cooked shrimps

2 cups pineapple chunks

½ cup sweet mixed pickles

3 tablespoons crystallized ginger, finely cut

¼ cup peanut oil or margarine

1 cup pineapple juice

¼ cup sugar

¼ cup vinegar

¼ cup pickle juice

1 tablespoon soya sauce

3 tablespoons cornstarch

½ cup water

1 green pepper, slivered

Combine shrimp, pineapple chunks, sweet pickle, ginger; heat for 2 minutes in peanut oil or margarine.

In a separate bowl, blend pineapple juice. sugar, vinegar, pickle juice, soya sauce, cornstarch and water. Add this sauce to shrimp mixture; cook until thick and clear. Add slivered green pepper and mix well.

Place shrimp in centre of platter. Surround with hot cooked rice.

BAKED RED SNAPPER

Serves 2

½ cup onion, chopped

1 green pepper, seeded and chopped

1 garlic clove, minced

1 cup small shrimp, fresh or tinned

2 tablespoons butter

1-2 pound red snapper, washed, salt and peppered

1 tomato, quartered

1 cup dry white wine

In a frying pan sauté onion, pepper, garlic and shrimp in butter; remove from heat.

Line bottom and sides of a casserole with foil wrap. Place snapper in lined dish, arrange tomatoes around fish; spoon shrimp mixture over fish. Pour wine over all.

Bake at 350°F for 30 minutes.

SALMON LOAF

Serves 4

2 eggs

½ cup milk

1 teaspoon salt

pepper

½ pound canned salmon, flaked

¾ cup cracker crumbs

2 tablespoons green pepper, chives or parsley

In a bowl beat eggs, milk, salt and pepper. Mix together all ingredients, pour into buttered casserole. Bake at 325°F for 1 hour.

Serve with Drawn Butter Sauce

Drawn Butter Sauce:

1 tablespoon butter

1 tablespoon flour

1 cup water

salt and pepper

1 hard-cooked egg, chopped

handful of chopped parsley

Melt butter, stir in flour. Slowly add water, salt and pepper. When thickened, add egg and chopped parsley.

CURRIED OYSTERS

Serves 4

1 pint oysters, with liquor

1/4 cup butter

1 small onion, grated

1/2 medium-sized apple, peeled and grated

2 tablespoons chutney

1 tablespoon flour

1/2 teaspoon curry powder

1/2 teaspoon salt

1/2 cup milk

4 cups cooked rice

Drain oysters, reserving liquor, add enough water to make 1/2 cup. In a skillet, melt butter, stir in onion, apple, chutney, flour, curry and salt.

Cook for 5 minutes over medium heat, stirring frequently. Add oyster liquor and milk; simmer 2 to 3 minutes. Add oysters and cook just until the edges begin to curl. Serve with hot rice.

Oysters with a difference — and that does not mean a pearl!

SEAFOOD QUICHE

Serves 4

1-9 inch unbaked pie shell

3 slices bacon

1 medium-sized onion, chopped

3 eggs

1 cup and "a bit of" cereal cream

1/2 teaspoon salt

1/2 teaspoon pepper

1/2 teaspoon sugar

1/2 teaspoon cayenne pepper

1/4 pound Swiss cheese, grated

1-6 ounce package frozen or canned crabmeat (thawed)

In a skillet, sauté and onion until cooked. Transfer to a large bowl and gently beat in the eggs, cream and seasonings. Stir in Swiss cheese and crabmeat. Pour into uncooked pie shell. Bake at 450°F for 12 minutes, lower heat and bake at 325° F for 35 minutes.

To double prepare the filling 1 1/2 times only.

LOBSTER AND RICE

Serves 8 to 10

1 pound fresh mushrooms, sliced

¼ cup butter

4-5 ounce cans lobster

4 cups cooked rice

2-10 ounce cans condensed cream of mushroom soup

¼ cup green onions, chopped

½ cup celery, chopped

salt and pepper to taste

2 cups sherry

1 cup Cheddar cheese, grated

In a frying pan sauté mushrooms in butter. Mix all ingredients together, except grated cheese. Pour into a large casserole dish, sprinkle with cheese and bake, uncovered at 350°F for 50 to 60 minutes.

Quick and easy!

STUFFED SALMON

Serves 6

1 fresh salmon, 4½ to 5 pounds

Stuffing:

½ cup chopped onion

1 cup diced celery

4 teaspoons lemon rind, grated

1 teaspoon paprika

4 tablespoons butter

½ cup sour cream

5 cups soft bread, cubed.

Bone the salmon; prepare stuffing. In a skillet, sauté onion and celery until tender. Stir in grated rind, paprika and sour cream; and bread cubes and blend well. Add sautéed onions and celery and mix thoroughly. Sprinkle inside of salmon cavity with salt; then loosely stuff cavity. Fasten with toothpicks or skewers; loop string around skewers as if lacing a shoe.

Place salmon in a large greased baking dish; brush with butter. Bake at 450°F 10 minutes for 1 inch thickness of fish.

4

Caviar Pie
Recipe on page 23

CRAB STUFFED EGGPLANT

Serves 4

2 medium-sized eggplants

1 cup crab meat (salt and pepper to taste)

4 to 6 tablespoons oil

2 medium onions, sliced

2 teaspoons paprika

1 tablespoon tomato paste

2 tomatoes, peeled, seeded, sliced

½ teaspoon oregano

pinch of cayenne

2 tablespoons grated Parmesan cheese

1 ½ tablespoons melted butter

Wipe eggplants, trim stems, cut in half lengthwise. Score cut surface with a knife, sprinkle with salt, leave 30 minutes.
Set oven at 350°F. Rinse eggplants with cold water to remove excess salt, and dry. Heat oil in a heavy pan, fry eggplant, cut side down, until brown. Bake 10 to 15 minutes on baking sheet in oven (or until tender)

Cook onions in remaining oil until soft. Add paprika, tomato paste, tomatoes, oregano, and cayenne. Season and cook until mixture is thick.

Scoop flesh from baked eggplants, reserving the shells. Add flesh to tomato mixture. Cook 2 to 3 minutes. Flake crab meat, add to pan and heat. Pile mixture into shells, sprinkle with cheese and melted butter. Bake at 425°F for 6 to 7 minutes.

For a change substitute crab meat with baby shrimps, mushrooms or chicken.

COCKTAIL SAUCE

Enough for 3 dozen large shrimps

1-3 ounce wine glass of ketchup
1-3 ounce wine glass of mayonnaise
1-3 ounce wine glass of whipped cream
4 tablespoons whiskey
2 tablespoons brandy
dash of Worcestershire sauce
salt to taste
shake of red pepper

Mix well. Chill. Serve. Enjoy!

BUTTERFLY SHRIMPS

Serves 4

1 pound uncooked shrimps
1/2 cup all-purpose flour
1 teaspoon baking powder
1 teaspoon salt
1 teaspoon accent
1 tablespoon lemon juice
2 egg whites
1/2 cup water
2 cups vegetable oil

Shell shrimps but leave the tail portion in the shell. Devein, wash and drain shrimps.

Batter:
Mix flour, baking powder, salt, accent and lemon juice with water. Beat egg whites until soft peaks are formed. Fold into flour mixture.

Coat each shrimp with batter, leaving tail uncoated. Deep fry in hot oil (375°F) a few at a time. Serve hot.

Vegetables

TURNIP SOUFFLE

Serves 6

1 medium-sized turnip, cooked and mashed

2 tablespoons flour

1 tablespoon brown sugar

2 tablespoons butter

2 eggs, beaten

1 tablespoon baking powder

½ teaspoon nutmeg

salt and pepper to taste

buttered bread crumbs

parsley

Combine all ingredients, except bread crumbs and parsley. Mix thoroughly. Place in a buttered soufflé dish.

Top with buttered bread crumbs. Bake at 375°F for 25 minutes. Garnish with parsley, just before serving.

GREEN BEANS À LA FROMAGE

Serves 6 to 8

1 pound mushrooms, sliced

1 onion, sliced

½ cup butter

½ cup flour

2 cups milk

1 cup cream

½ pound Cheddar cheese, grated

½ teaspoon Tabasco

1 teaspoon salt

½ teaspoon pepper

3-10 ounce packages French-style green beans

toasted almonds (optional)

In a large fry pan sauté mushrooms and onions in butter. Add flour; blend well. Slowly add milk and cream, stirring constantly until thick. Add cheese, Tabasco, salt and pepper.

Cook beans as directed on carton; drain well; place in oven-proof dish. Pour sauce over beans; add toasted almonds. Bake at 350°F for 1 hour.

GORD SINCLAIR'S SPECIAL TURNIP

Serves 4 to 6

1 turnip

2 saccarin tablets

butter

pepper

Actually see, what I'm famous for is my absolutely delicious turnip. Turnip of all things. But when Sinclair does the Turnip (note it is now capitalized!) even people who hate it . . . love it.

So what you do is you get a good waxed turnip, and you cut it into about one cubic inch squares, and you boil hell out of it . . . that means at least an hour.

The secret ingredient is TWO SACCHARIN TABLETS! They must be there while it is boiled.

Then you mash it with copious amounts of butter and liberal sprinklings of pepper so it is almost whipped; having salted it lightly before boiling of course.

It may not be a recipe per se, but by God it's great turnip and with a rare sirloin steak and fried onions, I can be a hero anytime.

ZUCCHINI WITH SHRIMPS

Serves 8

8 small zucchini

2 tablespoons butter

1 shallot, or scallion, finely chopped

1 teaspoon paprika

4 medium-sized tomatoes, peeled, seeded and chopped

salt and pepper

½ pound cooked, peeled small shrimp

2 tablespoons grated Parmesan cheese (for topping)

Mornay Sauce:

2 tablespoons butter

2 tablespoons flour

1 ¼ cups milk

¼ cup grated Parmesan cheese

½ teaspoon Dijon-style mustard

Wash zucchini and trim each end, but do not peel. Blanch by boiling whole in salted water for 5 minutes, draining and refreshing in cold water. Cut a thin lengthwise slice from each zucchini, carefully scoop out flesh with point of a teaspoon and chop.

Melt butter in a saucepan; add shallot and cook, covered, over low heat, until soft but not brown; add paprika, chopped zucchini flesh and tomatoes. Cook briskly for 2 to 3 minutes. Season with salt and pepper. Stir in the shrimps. Arrange zucchini cases in a buttered oval baking dish and fill with tomato and shrimp mixture.

Mornay sauce: Melt butter in a saucepan; stir in flour and when foaming remove from heat and stir in milk. Bring to a boil, stirring until sauce thickens. Simmer 2 to 3 minutes, remove from heat, stir in cheese and mustard. Season to taste and reheat, if necessary, without boiling.

Spoon Mornay sauce over the zucchini; sprinkle with cheese and bake in a hot oven (425°F) for 10 minutes or until brown.

Note: If you feel you would like to have more sauce, double the Mornay recipe.

EGGPLANT PARMIGIANA

Serves 6

½ cup chopped onion

1 clove garlic, crushed

1 pound ground chuck beef

2 tablespoons butter

1-19 ounce can, Italian tomatoes (undrained)

1-6 ounce can tomato paste

2 teaspoons dried oregano

1 teaspoon dried basil

1 ½ teaspoons salt

¼ teaspoon pepper

1 tablespoon brown sugar

1 cup boiling water

1 eggplant (large) (1 to 1 ½ pounds)

2 eggs, slightly beaten

½ cup dry bread crumbs

1 ½ cups grated Parmesan cheese

⅓ cup salad oil

1-8 ounce package Mozzarella cheese, sliced

Lightly grease 13 x 9 x 2 inch baking dish. In large skillet sauté onion, garlic and chuck in butter for about 5 minutes. Add tomatoes, tomato paste, oregano, basil, salt, pepper, sugar and 1 cup water; bring to boil. Reduce heat; simmer uncovered for 20 minutes.

Wash eggplant, do not peel. Cut crosswise into slices inch thick. In pie plate, combine eggs and 1 tablespoon water; mix well.
On a sheet of wax paper, combine bread crumbs with ½ cup Parmesan cheese. Mix thoroughly. Dip eggplant slices into egg mixture, coating well; then dip into crumb mixture, coating evenly.

Sauté eggplant slices, a few at a time in 1 tablespoon hot oil until golden-brown and crisp on both sides. Add more oil as needed.

Arrange half the eggplant slices in bottom of prepared baking dish. Sprinkle with half remaining Parmesan cheese. Top with half of the Mozzarella cheese. Cover with half the tomato sauce.

Arrange remaining eggplant slices over the tomato sauce. Cover with rest of the Parmesan, tomato sauce and Mozzarella.

Bake at 350°F uncovered for 25 minutes.

ONION CASSEROLE

Serves 6

6 large onions

1 cup thick white sauce

1/2 cup grated Cheddar cheese

1/2 cup mushrooms, fresh or canned

1/2 cup bread crumbs

Peel and slice onions crosswise in thin slices. Cook onions in boiling water until tender; drain.

Add cheese and mushrooms to the white sauce.

In a greased casserole dish, place a layer of onions; cover with some of the sauce. Repeat.

Top with buttered bread crumbs and bake in 350°F oven for 1/2 hour.

Can be made the day before.

Excellent with a roast.

SCALLOPED TOMATOES AND ONIONS

Serves 5 to 8

8 medium onions

8 tomatoes

salt and pepper

1 tablespoon sugar

1 1/4 cups soft bread cubes

1/4 cup chopped parsley

1 1/4 cups light cream

2/3 cup dry bread crumbs

1/3 cup grated Parmesan cheese

2 tablespoons butter

Slice onions very thinly. Put them in a bowl and add boiling water to cover; let stand 3 minutes; drain well. Peel tomatoes and cut into thick slices.

In a buttered 2 quart casserole put a layer of tomato slices; sprinkle generously with salt and pepper and with some sugar. Add a layer of onions, some salt, bread cubes and some parsley. Repeat layers until everything is used up. Pour light cream over top.

Combine bread crumbs and cheese and sprinkle over top. Pat with butter. Bake 45 minutes at 350°F.

CARROTS EN CASSEROLE

Serves 6

1 pound carrots

1 cup golden raisins

1 cup water

1 teaspoon salt

½ cup brown sugar

4 tablespoons butter

2 tablespoons lemon juice

Cut carrots diagonally in thin slices. Place raisins, water, salt and carrots in saucepan and heat to boiling. Simmer 30 minutes. Drain.

Place in a casserole, sprinkle with sugar, dot with butter and add lemon juice. Bake in a slow oven, 325°F uncovered, for 30 minutes.

CHEESE SCALLOPED CARROTS

Serves 8 to 10

12 medium sized carrots, sliced

1 small onion, minced

¼ cup butter

¼ cup flour

1 teaspoon salt

½ teaspoon pepper

¼ teaspoon dry mustard

¼ teaspoon celery salt

2 cups milk

½ pound sharp cheese, sliced

⅓ cup bread crumbs, buttered

Parboil carrots until barely tender, in salted water and drain. Sauté onion in butter in a frying pan for 2 or 3 minutes. Stir in flour, salt and pepper, mustard and celery salt. Add milk; cook slowly, stirring until smooth.

In a 2 quart casserole dish place a layer of carrots, then cheese. Repeat. Pour over sauce; top with buttered crumbs. Bake, uncovered for 45 minutes at 350°F.

Can be made the day before.

BROCCOLI CASSEROLE

Serves 6 to 8

2-10-ounce packages frozen broccoli

1-10-ounce can cream of chicken soup

1 tablespoon flour

½ cup sour cream

¼ cup grated carrot

1 onion, chopped

Topping: packaged stuffing mix, 4 tablespoons butter.

Cook broccoli; drain well; place in a 2 quart casserole. In a saucepan slowly add chicken soup to flour. Stir in sour cream, grated carrot, and chopped onion. Pour over broccoli; cover with topping. Bake at 350°F for 35 minutes.

BRAISED HERBED CUCUMBER

Serves 6 to 8

10 firm cucumbers

1 tablespoon coarse salt

1 tablespoon white wine vinegar

¼ cup butter

2 tablespoons minced fresh dill

2 tablespoons minced fresh chives

1 tablespoons minced shallots

white pepper

salt

½ cup heavy cream

minced parsley (optional)

more minced dill (optional)

Peel firm cucumbers, half them lengthwise and, with a small spoon, scoop out the seeds. Cut the cucumbers into pieces, 1/3 inch wide and 1¼ inches long and place in a bowl. Sprinkle with coarse salt, white wine vinegar and let stand at room temperature for 2 to 3 hours.

Drain cucumbers in a colander and pat dry. Transfer the cucumbers to a flameproof dish; toss with melted butter, fresh dill, chives, minced shallots, white pepper and salt to taste. Bake in a preheated moderate oven 375°F for 25 minutes or until barely tender.

Remove the dish from the oven and add heavy cream. Toss the cucumbers with the cream over moderate high heat for 5 minutes or until the cream is reduced and thickened. Sprinkle with minced parsley and more minced dill, if desired.

CHOW YUK

Serves 4 to 6

8 ounces snow pea pods

1 bunch broccoli, stems and tops (approximately 1 pound)

½ cup sliced water chestnuts

½ cup sliced green onions

1 tablespoon fresh ginger

½ cup mushrooms

2 tablespoons peanut oil

2 tablespoons soya sauce

3 tablespoons dry sherry

Slice broccoli, water chestnuts, green onions, ginger and mushrooms early in day; cover and refrigerate until ready to cook.

Heat peanut oil in frying pan or wok. Sauté ginger for 2 minutes. Add broccoli and water chestnuts. Stir in soya sauce and sherry. Cook 2 to 3 minutes, stirring occasionally. Add pea pods, mushrooms and green onions, stirring until heated through.

Serve with fried rice.

RATATOUILLE

Serves 4 to 6

2 medium zucchini, thinly sliced

1 small eggplant, peeled, sliced ¼ inch thick

1 large green pepper, seeded, cut into strips

2 medium-sized onions, coarsely chopped

1-16 ounce can tomato and mushroom sauce

½ pound fresh mushrooms, sliced

1 garlic clove, crushed

¼ teaspoon oregano

½ teaspoon salt

4 slices Swiss cheese

chopped parsley

Prepare vegetables. Combine vegetables with sauce, fresh mushrooms, garlic and other seasonings in a large skillet. Cover; simmer until tender, about 20 to 25 minutes. Pour into a casserole dish, cover with sliced cheese. Bake at 350°F for 15 minutes. Garnish with parsley.

Quick and easy!

WHIPPED POTATOES

Serves 10 to 12

9 medium-sized to large potatoes

1-8 ounce package cream cheese, softened

1 cup sour cream

2 teaspoons onion salt

1 teaspoon salt

pinch of white pepper

2 tablespoons butter

Cook potatoes and mash well. Add all remaining ingredients and beat thoroughly. Place in a large buttered casserole dish. Dot with butter. Bake at 350°F for 30 minutes.

If preparing ahead, cover with plastic wrap and refrigerate or freeze. Thaw before baking.

Easy and different!

CORN STUFFED ONIONS

Serves 6

6 medium sized onions

1-12 ounce can whole kernel corn, drained

2 tablespoons butter or margarine

2 tablespoons all-purpose flour

½ teaspoon salt

dash pepper

1 cup milk

2 tablespoons chopped pimientos

1 cup (4 ounces) shredded processed American cheese

Hollow onions; chop centers to make 1 cup. Fill onions with corn; set aside remaining corn.

Place onions in 9 x 9 x 2 inch baking pan. Add 2 tablespoons water; cover. Bake in 400°F oven for 1 hour. Cook chopped onion in butter or margarine; stir in flour, salt and pepper. Add milk; cook and stir until thickened. Add reserved corn and pimientos.

Return to boiling; stir in cheese until melted. Place onions in serving dish, spoon on sauce.

ITALIAN ZUCCHINI

Serves 4 to 6

8 small zucchini

6 medium-sized tomatoes

2 medium-sized onions, finely chopped

2 tablespoons vegetable oil

salt and pepper to taste

1/4 teaspoon oregano

Wash and cut zucchini into 1 inch cubes. Coarsely chop tomatoes. Sauté chopped onion in vegetable oil in a skillet until transparent, but not brown. Add zucchini, tomatoes, seasonings; cook gently for 10 minutes.

Superb "perk" for a vegetable with cold meats.

ZUCCHINI – TOMATO PIE

Serves 12

2-9 inch pie shells, partially baked, until lightly browned

1/2 large onion, sliced

3 tablespoons olive oil

1 pound zucchini, thinly sliced

2 cloves garlic, minced

1-14 1/2 ounce can tomatoes

1-8 ounce can tomato sauce

1/2 teaspoon oregano, crumbled

1/2 teaspoon basil, crumbled

salt and fresh ground pepper to taste

2 cups Ricotta cheese

3 eggs beaten

1/2 cup milk

8 ounces Mozzarella cheese, shredded

1/2 cup grated Parmesan cheese

Preheat oven to 375°F. Sauté onion in oil until transparent. Add zucchini and sauté approximately 5 minutes or until tender but crisp. Remove from pan and set aside.

Add garlic, tomatoes, tomato sauce and seasonings to pan. Cook over medium-high heat, stirring occasionally, until reduced to 2 cups. Set aside.

Beat Ricotta with eggs and milk and set aside. Spoon zucchini mixture into bottom of each pie shell. Pour 1/4 cup tomato mixture over each shell and top with Riccota mixture.

Bake for 40 minutes. Spread remaining tomato mixture over pies and top with Mozzarella and Parmesan cheese. Bake for 7 to 8 minutes longer.

ONION CUSTARD

Serves 6

¼ cup butter

6 medium-sized onions, sliced and diced

2 eggs, beaten

1 cup milk

1 teaspoon salt

pinch of pepper

pinch of nutmeg or curry powder

In a frying pan melt butter, add onions; stir until well-coated with butter and sauté until golden brown. Combine remaining ingredients, and add to onions. Pour into a buttered one quart casserole dish. Bake, uncovered, at 375°F for 25 to 30 minutes or until set like a custard.

Excellent with seafood, veal or fowl.

EGGPLANT CASSEROLE

Serves 4

1 eggplant, sliced and cooked

3 tablespoons butter

1 medium-sized onion, chopped

3 tablespoons flour

1-14 ounce can tomatoes or 3 large tomatoes

1 teaspoon salt

1 tablespoon brown sugar

1 cup grated Cheddar cheese

½ cup bread crumbs

Arrange eggplant in a buttered casserole dish. Melt butter in frying pan; sauté onions. Blend in flour; add tomatoes, salt, sugar. Pour sauce over eggplant. Cover with cheese, sprinkle with bread crumbs.

Bake at 350°F for 30 minutes.

CREAMED SPINACH AND MADEIRA

Serves 8

4 pounds spinach

1/4 cup water

pinch of salt

3 tablespoons butter

dash of nutmeg

salt and pepper

1/2 cup heavy cream

1/2 pound sliced mushrooms

2 tablespoons butter

1/4 cup Madeira

Cook spinach in water for about 10 minutes, or until soft. Drain thoroughly; put through finest blade of meat grinder. Drain again and add 3 tablespoons butter, dash of nutmeg, salt, pepper and heavy cream.

Sauté mushrooms in butter for 4 to 5 minutes, add to spinach and stir in Madeira. Re-heat briefly and serve.

This always receives compliments.

WILD RICE ALMONDINE

Serves 6

2 cups wild rice

1/2 cup olive oil or butter

2 tablespoons chopped onion

2 tablespoons chopped chives

2 tablespoons chopped shallots

3 tablespoons chopped green pepper

4 1/2 cups chicken broth

salt and pepper to taste

3/4 cup shredded almonds

Wash wild rice in several baths of cold water and drain. Heat olive oil (or butter) stir in onion, chives, shallots and green pepper. Sauté.

Add rice; cook over a very gentle heat, stirring constantly until rice begins to turn yellowish. Add heated chicken broth. Salt and pepper to taste. Stir in shredded almonds.

Turn into an uncovered casserole and bake in a medium oven at 325°F for 1 to 1 1/2 hours.

SPANISH RICE

Serves 4 to 6

3 tablespoons butter
1 pound mushrooms, sliced
¾ cup long-grained rice, washed
¾ cup onion, chopped
1 cup celery, chopped
1-19 ounce can tomatoes
2 green peppers, seeded and diced
1 pimiento, diced
1 teaspoon salt
dash of Worcestershire

Lightly sauté mushrooms in butter. Combine all ingredients; bake in an uncovered casserole dish at 325°F for 1½ hours.

GREEN AND YELLOW RICE

Serves 6

3 cups cooked rice
¼ cup butter
4 eggs, beaten
1 pound sharp Cheddar cheese, grated
1 cup milk
1-10 ounce package frozen spinach, cooked, drained and chopped
1 tablespoon chopped onion
1 tablespoon Worcestershire sauce
½ teaspoon marjoram
½ teaspoon thyme
½ teaspoon salt
¼ teaspoon rosemary

Prepare rice. Melt butter, add to rice. Set aside. Beat eggs and grate cheese. Add milk to eggs; then stir in cheese, spinach and mix well. Stir in onion, seasonings; combine entire mixture with rice. Place in a 2 quart casserole dish. Set in a pan of water in a 350°F oven and bake uncovered for 45 minutes.

Crêpes, Eggs and Cheese

SWISS PIE WITH CRABMEAT SAUCE

Serves 8

1 unbaked 9 inch pie shell

4 slightly beaten egg yolks

1 ½ cups light cream

½ teaspoon salt

⅛ teaspoon ground nutmeg

4 egg whites

6 ounces (1 ½ cups) natural Swiss cheese, shredded

Bake pie shell at 450°F for 7 minutes, remove. Reduce temperature to 350°F. Combine egg yolks, cream, salt and nutmeg.

Beat egg whites until stiff, fold into yolk mixture. Fold in cheese, pour into pie shell.

Bake at 350°F for 40 to 45 minutes or until a knife inserted into the centre comes out clean. Let stand 5 minutes. Serve with crabmeat sauce.

CRABMEAT SAUCE

Sauté 1 cup (7½ ounce can) crabmeat, drained and flaked in 2 tablespoons butter. Blend in 2 teaspoons flour and ⅛ teaspoon salt. Add 1 cup light cream; cook and stir until thickened.

A delightful luncheon dish, or for Sunday Brunch.

PATRICK MARTIN'S CHEESE FONDUE

I acquired this recipe a few years ago while living in a small mountain village in Switzerland. It's never failed me and I've never tasted better.

½ pound Gruyère cheese

½ pound Emmenthal cheese

½ pound Swiss "Bagne" cheese (also known as Raclette)

1 heaping tablespoon cornstarch

1 large clove garlic

12 to 14 ounces of a light white wine (not too dry)

One French stick cut into 1 inch cubes (and left out to dry for a few hours)

2 ounces kirsch (if a liqueur, similar to kirsch but made from apples can be found, it is preferred)

nutmeg

black pepper

Shred cheese, toss together with cornstarch. Rub fondue dish with garlic. Heat the wine in the dish over a medium high temperature until tiny bubbles form. Turn heat to low. Add cheese gradually, stirring constantly. When all cheese is melted and mixture is constant, add ½ to 1 ounce of kirsch. Stir in nutmeg to taste. Grind in black pepper as you serve it. Dip bread cubes into the mixture for a delightful meal!!!

Serve with pickled onions, or a light salad. For added zest, try dipping the bread first into the leftover kirsch, then into the cheese.

Remember two Swiss customs which must be faithfully observed when eating this dish:

1 The treasured part of the meal is the "souer" or "nun", the crust which forms at the bottom of the dish. Use low heat, so not to burn. Give this crust to an honoured guest, or share it among the group. (It should lift off with a fork).

2 The Swiss are very neat, orderly people. Anyone who drops his bread into the cheese must pay a penalty: either a bottle of wine for the table or a kiss to everyone of the opposite sex.

BRUNCH EGG CASSEROLE

Serves 8

(Make 2 days in advance)

8 eggs

4 cups milk

10 slices bread, well-buttered and cubed

½ pound Cheddar cheese, grated

1 teaspoon dry mustard

2 tablespoons curry powder

salt and pepper to taste

Lightly beat eggs and milk. In an ungreased casserole, alternate layers of cheese and bread cubes. Stir seasonings into eggs and milk, pour entire mixture over cheese and bread. Cover and refrigerate for 48 hours. Remove from refrigerator ½ hour before baking. Bake at 350°F for 40 minutes.

This makes a wonderful breakfast for a crowd of weekend guests, served with juice and a sweet roll. A pound of cooked sausages, mushrooms or asparagus layered on top makes a perfect final touch.

CHEESE SOUFFLE

Serves 4

1 thin slice white bread, torn

½ teaspoon dry mustard

¼ teaspoon salt

dash cayenne

3 tablespoons soft butter, or margarine

1 cup hot milk

1 cup diced Cheddar cheese

4 egg yolks

4 egg whites

Into blender put bread, mustard, salt and cayenne. Cover and blend for 5 seconds (my button 6, purée). Remove cover, add butter, hot milk (I usually soften the hard butter by adding it to the hot milk and letting it stand for a little while), cheese and egg yolks and blend for another 25 seconds. In 1½ quart soufflé dish (larger dish required for the larger quantity), beat egg whites until stiff.

Pour cheese mixture over egg whites and fold in until lightly blended.

Bake in pre-heated oven at 375°F for 35 minutes. This soufflé rises beautifully.

This quantity is fine as a starter for four people; if used as a main, light supper dish for 4, increase quantitites by half again, cooking time is the same.

A never, never fail blender recipe.

DINAH CHRISTIE'S M'EGGS (My Eggs)

Just lightly fry your eggs in butter, covering them after they have been seasoned. While the yolks are still soft, dot them with sour cream and sprinkle them with grated Parmesan cheese. Then place them under the broiler for 2 to 3 minutes until golden and gurgling.

It makes a pleasant change.

QUICHE LORRAINE

Serves 6

1-9 inch unbaked pie shell

8 slices bacon, fried and crumbled

½ pound Swiss cheese

1 tablespoon flour

½ teaspoon salt

½ teaspoon nutmeg

3 beaten eggs

1¾ cups milk

Bake pie shell 7 minutes at 450°F; remove from oven

Reduce heat to 325°F.

Put bacon and cheese in the pie shell. Beat togethher flour, salt, nutmeg, eggs and milk. Pour into shell. Bake 35 to 40 minutes.

Cool for 25 minutes.

ONION QUICHE

Serves 8

2 to 4 onions, medium-sized

5 ounces butter

1 tablespoon flour

3 eggs

½ cup cream

½ cup milk

freshly ground pepper to taste

nutmeg to taste

salt to taste

9 inch unbaked pie shell

Chop onions finely and sauté in butter until transparent.

Mix thoroughly flour, eggs, cream and milk. Add pepper, nutmeg and salt. Stir in onions. Pour into pie shell and bake at 375°F for 30 to 40 minutes.

MACARONI AND CHEESE BAKE *Serves 8*

1-7 ounce package macaroni, cooked and drained

2 cups creamed cottage cheese

2 cups sour cream

1 egg, slightly beaten

2 cups Cheddar cheese, grated

salt and pepper to taste

½ cup bread crumbs

paprika

Mix all ingredients well and pour into buttered casserole dish. Top with bread crumbs, dot with butter and sprinkle with paprika. Bake at 350°F for 45 minutes.
Slightly different from the norm!

SAUSAGE AND ONION QUICHE *Serves 6 to 8*

½ pound sausage meat

3 tablespoons butter

5 medium-sized onions, chopped (approximately 3 cups)

3 eggs

½ pint whipping cream

2 tablespoons Dijon mustard (or ¼ teaspoon dry mustard)

nutmeg, salt and pepper to taste

1 cup Swiss cheese, grated

1-9 inch pie shell, baked

Preheat oven to 350°F. In a heavy skillet, cook sausage meat while continually crumbling with a fork. Remove sausage meat and drain well. Add butter to sausage fat in skillet; sauté onions until golden. Remove onions with a slotted spoon and drain. Cover pie shell with sausage meat and onions. In a bowl whisk together eggs, cream, mustard and seasonings. Stir in cheese. Pour into pie shell and bake at 350°F for 35 minutes.

EGG AND TUNA MOUSSE

Serves 6

2-7 ounce cans tuna, drained, and flaked
3 hard-cooked eggs, chopped
2 large tomatoes, skinned and chopped
salt and pepper to taste
pinch of chopped chives
pinch of chopped parsley
1 teaspoon anchovy paste
½ teaspoon Worcestershire sauce
lemon juice to taste
2 teaspoons gelatine
½ - 10 ounce can consommé
½ pint whipping cream, whipped

In a large bowl, mix flaked tuna, eggs and tomatoes; add seasonings. Do not mash as the consistency should be coarse. In a small saucepan sprinkle gelatine over consommé and let stand for 5 minutes; then heat until gelatine is completely dissolved. Set aside and allow to cool. When cool stir consommé mixture into bowl with tuna. Fold whipped cream into entire mixture and pour into a souffle dish or 1 quart mould. Refrigerate.

BASIC CRÊPES

Makes 12 Crêpes

3/4 cup flour

1/8 teaspoon salt

3 eggs, beaten

2 tablespoons melted butter

3/4 cup milk (approximately)

sweet butter

Sift flour and salt into a bowl; add beaten eggs and beat with a wire whisk until smooth. Add melted butter and mix thoroughly. Add enough milk until the batter has the consistency of heavy cream. Let stand for at least 30 minutes; then beat again.

Heat a 6 or 7 inch pan and brush with sweet butter. Pour in about 2 teaspoons of batter to cover the bottom of the pan.

When the crêpes brown (about 2 minutes) loosen, turn until golden on the second side.

These may be frozen between pieces of waxed paper. They may be filled for an entrée or used as an elegant dessert dish.

GREEN HERB CRÊPES

Add 1/3 cup chopped fresh dill weed, parsley or scallions to crêpe batter in blender. Blend at high speed 1 minute until it is a pale green-flecked cream.

DESSERT CRÊPES

Yields approximately 20 - 7 inch Crêpes.

1 cup all-purpose flour, sifted

4 large eggs

1 1/2 cups milk

1 tablespoon granulated sugar

2 tablespoons orange-flavored liqueur

1/4 cup unsalted butter, melted and cooled.

In blender in the following order, place flour, eggs, milk, sugar and liqueur. Cover and blend at medium speed. Stop and scrape sides down often. When batter is smooth, add butter and blend again.

CHOCOLATE CRÊPES

Just before cooking, stir into dessert crêpe batter 2 ounces finely chopped semi-sweet chocolate, 1 teaspoon vanilla and 1/4 teaspoon salt.

SUGGESTED CRÊPE FILLINGS

Marbella

Serves 6

2 tablespoons oil

1 ½ teaspoons minced garlic

2 green peppers, seeded, diced

1-2 pound 3 ounce can whole peeled tomatoes, drained

½ pound Kielbasa sausage, sliced

½ cup pitted ripe Greek olives or

pimiento stuffed olives

½ teaspoon salt

dash of crushed hot red pepper

½ cup chopped fresh parsley

¾ cup grated Parmesan cheese

12 entrée crêpes

In a large skillet heat oil over moderate heat. Add garlic and cook 30 seconds. Add peppers and cook 3 minutes, stirring often. Add tomatoes and cook 5 minutes, until most of the tomato liquid has evaporated. Add remaining ingredients except parsley, crêpes and cheese.

Simmer covered 20 minutes or until thick. Stir in parsley. Use ¼ cup filling and ½ tablespoon of cheese for each crêpe. Transfer filled crêpes to a 14 X 9 X 2 inch baking dish. Sprinkle with remaining cheese.

Cover and bake 30 minutes at 325°F until cheese is melted and crêpes are hot. Heat broiler. Uncover baking dish and broil until cheese is lightly brown.

Salmon and Sour Cream

Serves 6

Best with green-herb crêpes

3 cups sour cream

¾ cup minced scallions

3 or 4 - 7 ounce cans salmon, drained and flaked

½ cup lightly salted butter, melted

lemon quarters

12 green herb crêpes

Onto hot crêpe drizzle a little butter, spoon in some salmon and sprinkle with lemon juice and a dollop of sour cream.

Roll crêpe and top with another spoonful of sour cream mixture.

Apricot-Chocolate

Serves 8

16-7 inch hot chocolate crêpes

apricot preserve

½ pint heavy cream, whipped

chocolate curls

Apricot

½ pound dried apricot halves

1 ¼ cups water

¼ cup granulated sugar

In a small saucepan, bring apricots and water to a boil over high heat. Reduce heat to low, cover and simmer 30 minutes until fruit is very tender. Stir in sugar, gently mashing fruit to a lumpy purée.

Will keep several weeks in refrigerator in a tightly covered container.

Filling should be at room temperature before filling crêpes. Spread each crêpe with a generous tablespoon of apricot preserve. Fold crêpe in half and then half again.

Top each serving with whipped cream and chocolate curls.

Brandy Alexander

Makes 12

1 envelope unflavoured gelatine

¼ cup cold water

⅔ cup sugar

dash salt

3 eggs, separated

⅓ cup brandy

⅓ cup dark crème de cacao

12 dessert crêpes

Sprinkle the gelatine over water in a small saucepan to soften. Add ⅓ cup of sugar, salt, egg yolks. Cook and stir over low heat until the mixture begins to thicken, about 5 minutes.

Remove the pan from the heat; add brandy and crême de cacao. Chill until syrupy, stirring occasionally.

Beat the egg whites until soft peaks form. Gradually add the remaining ⅓ cup sugar and beat to stiff peaks. Fold in the gelatine mixture along with the whipped cream.

Place about ¼ cup of filling in the center of each crêpe. Fold cornucopia style. Serve with additional whipped cream.

Brandied Chicken

Serves 6

2 shallots, finely chopped

½ pound mushrooms, sliced

2 tablespoons butter

2 tablespoons brandy

½ cup white wine

2 tablespoons tomato paste

2 chicken bouillon cubes, crushed

1 cup boiling water

2 cups cooked chicken, cubed

12 crêpes

Sauté shallots and mushrooms in butter until tender. Add the brandy and wine. Simmer until a liquid is reduced to half.

Stir in tomato paste, bouillon and water. Simmer the sauce to reduce it by about a third. Add the chicken.

Fill each crêpe with about ¼ cup filling. Roll up or fold. Serve immediately.

Desserts

COFFEE MOUSSE

Serves 6

22 large marshmallows

1/2 cup strong coffee

1/2 pint whipping cream

1/2 package ladyfingers

Melt marshmallows and coffee in double boiler top. Cool. Add stiffly whipped cream. Line serving bowl with ladyfingers. Pour mixture over ladyfingers and chill for several hours.

This recipe doubles easily for 12 servings or second helpings.

STRAWBERRY BUTTER CRUNCH CROWN

Serves 12

1/2 cup butter

1/4 cup brown sugar (packed)

1 cup sifted flour

1/2 cup chopped pecans or walnuts

1 envelope unflavored gelatine (1 tablespoon)

1/2 cup cold water

2 pints strawberries, halved

1 teaspoon lemon juice

3/4 cup sugar

few drops red food colouring

1 cup whipping cream, whipped

Heat oven to 400°F. Mix butter, brown sugar, flour and nuts with hands. Spread in oblong pan, 13 x 9 1/2 x 2 inch. Bake 15 minutes. Stir baked crumbs with spoon. COOL.

Soften gelatine in cold water. Mash 1 cup of the strawberries in saucepan. Add lemon juice and sugar. Bring to a boil, stirring occasionally. Remove from heat, stir in gelatine until dissolved; add few drops of red food colouring. Dip a few uncooked berry halves in this mixture and place on bottom of mould to form an attractive design. Chill rest of mixture until partially set. Fold in remaining berries and whipped cream.

Fill mould in layers by alternating the berry mixture and crumb mixture, starting with berry mixture and ending with crumbs. (Make about 4 layers of each.) Chill.

Unmould by running a knife around bottom edge of mould; then dip in hot water for a few seconds. Garnish with strawberries.

May be made a day ahead of time.

MICKIE MOORE'S STRAWBERRY MOULD

Serves 8 to 10

3-3 ounce packages strawberry Jello

3 cups boiling water

1 envelope gelatine

½ cup cold water

1-19 ounce can crushed pineapple, undrained

1-10 ounce package frozen sliced strawberries, thawed

4 large bananas (mashed)

1 teaspoon lemon juice

1 pint THICK sour cream

Dissolve strawberry Jello with 3 cups boiling water. Dissolve gelatine in ½ cup cold water, then add to Jello mixture. Add pineapple, sliced strawberries, and mashed bananas. Use all liquid from pineapple and strawberries. Taste. If too sweet, add a teaspoon lemon juice.

Rinse out large mould with ice water. Place half the mixture in mould and put in refrigerator. When it sets, add a layer of THICK sour cream. Let set. Add rest of mixture, for third layer. Let set.

Unmould and decorate with fresh strawberries around edges.

WALNUT ROLL

Serves 6 to 8

7 eggs (separated)

¾ cup sugar

1 ½ cups ground walnuts

1 teaspoon baking powder

sifted icing sugar

1 cup heavy whipping cream

1 teaspoon vanilla

confectioners' sugar

Brush a 10 x 15 inch jelly-roll pan with oil; line it with waxed paper, and oil the paper. In a large bowl, beat the egg yolks with the sugar until the mixture is pale in colour and thick enough to "ribbon". Beat in the ground walnuts and baking powder. In a separate bowl, beat the egg whites until stiff; then fold into egg yolk mixture.

Spread batter into the prepared pan and bake at 350°F for 15 to 20 minutes, or until golden.

Cool the cake in the pan, cover with a damp towl and chill. Dust the cold cake generously with sifted confectioners' sugar and turn it out on a board covered with two overlapping sheets of wax paper. Carefully strip the paper from the bottom of the cake. Spread the cake with 1 cup whipping cream, whipped and flavoured with sugar and vanilla to taste. Roll up the cake, using the paper as an aid, and slide the roll onto a platter. Spread the roll with more sifted confectioners' sugar.

CHOCOLATE CUPS

Makes 9; medium 12 to 14

9 ounces semi-sweet chocolate

3 tablespoons butter

9 paper baking cups (fluted, large size)

Filling:

½ pint heavy cream

1-10 ounce can chocolate syrup

brandy or rum to taste

grated bitter chocolate

5

Chocolate Cups
Recipe on page 160

No-Bake Marbled Cheesecake
Recipe on page 161

Walnut Roll
Recipe on page 160

Melt chocolate in the top of a double boiler over barely simmering water. Remove from stove when chocolate is melted. Add butter and stir with a wire whisk until well blended.

Place paper cups in a muffin tin. Spoon chocolate into each cup, enough to cover bottom and crinkly sides (use back of spoon to press into crevices) until entire surface of cup is thinly coated. Refrigerate until hard about 14 to 20 minutes. Spoon in more chocolate covering sides and bottom. Repeat process until all chocolate is used. This part can be made days ahead and kept in the refrigerator.

Filling Whip cream until very stiff; add chocolate syrup and liquor to taste. Gently peel paper from chocolate cups (by pulling down a narrow strip from the top and then running it off sidewise). Arrange cups on a platter and spoon in filling. Sprinkle with grated chocolate and return to refrigerator until ready to serve.

NO-BAKE MARBLED CHEESECAKE

Serves 14 to 16

$1\frac{1}{3}$ cups graham-cracker crumbs, or vanilla-wafer crumbs

$2\frac{1}{4}$ cups sugar

$\frac{1}{4}$ cup melted butter

1 envelope gelatine

1-4 ounce package chocolate-flavour whipped dessert mix

3-8 ounce packages cream cheese, softened

$\frac{1}{8}$ teaspoon cinnamon

1-$3\frac{1}{4}$ ounce package vanilla-flavour whipped dessert mix

grated peel of 1 lemon

In medium bowl, mix wafer crumbs, $\frac{1}{4}$ cup sugar and melted butter. Press mixture firmly in bottom of 9 inch or 10 inch springform pan.

In measuring cup, sprinkle gelatine over $\frac{1}{4}$ cup cold water; place cup in small saucepan of hot water over medium heat and stir until gelatine is dissolved.

Prepare chocolate whipped-dessert mix as label directs; set aside. In large bowl with electric mixer, beat $1\frac{1}{2}$ packages cream cheese and 1 cup sugar until smooth; then beat in chocolate mixture along with 2 tablespoons melted gelatine and cinnamon until just blended; set aside.

Quickly prepare vanilla whipped-dessert mix as label directs; set aside. In large bowl with electric mixer at medium speed, beat remaining cream cheese and 1 cup sugar until smooth; then beat in vanilla mixture along with remaining melted gelatine and grated lemon peel until just blended.

Using two large spoons, alternately drop chocolate and vanilla mixtures evenly onto crumb crust. Using tip of knife, lightly score top surface in a crisscross pattern. Chill until firm, at least 6 hours.

To serve: With spatula loosen edge of cheesecake from pan; carefully remove sides of spring-form pan.

FROZEN MOUSSE WITH KIRSCH

Serves 6

(Make the day before)

1) Meringues:

2 egg whites

1/8 teaspoon cream of tartar

pinch of salt

1/2 cup sugar

1/2 teaspoon vanilla

In a bowl beat egg whites with cream of tartar and salt until they hold soft peaks. Continue beating and gradually add sugar, one tablespoonful at a time until mixture holds stiff peaks. Fold in vanilla.

Butter a cookie sheet; cover cookie sheet with buttered wax paper. Drop meringue on paper in 4 equal mounds and smooth each mound into 1/2 inch thickness.

Bake at 270°F for 50 minutes; until completely dry. Remove paper from cookie sheet; meringues from paper; cool on a rack.

2) Mousse:

1 cup whipping cream

2 tablespoons sugar

2 tablespoons kirsch

Whip cream, with sugar, until it holds stiff peaks. Break each meringue into 5 or 6 pieces; fold into whipped cream. Fold in kirsch. Pour into lightly oiled 1 quart mould. Cover with foil; freeze overnight.

Remove 20 minutes before serving. Serve with melba sauce.

3) Sauce:

1-10 ounce package frozen raspberries

1/4 cup confectioners' sugar

2 tablespoons kirsch

Thaw raspberries; strain and reserve syrup. Force berries through a fine sieve. Gradually stir in sugar; add kirsch; mix thoroughly and chill.

CHOCOLATE-GLAZED ÉCLAIRS

Makes 10

A typically French dessert, éclairs have become a Canadian favourite too and are not difficult to make at home. Based on chou paste (pâte à chou) which is also used for cream puffs, éclairs should have a lightly browned, crisp and tender shell with a slightly moist hollow interior. Usually filled with vanilla or chocolate custard, they also can be filled with sweetened whipped cream or ice cream, and can be glazed or unglazed.

¼ cup butter or margarine

1 cup water

¼ teaspoon salt

1 cup all-purpose flour

4 eggs

1-3 or 3¼ ounce package vanilla pudding mix

¼ teaspoon almond extract

1 cup heavy cream, whipped

chocolate glaze

To make chou paste:

Preheat oven to 375°F. Grease large cookie sheet. In a 3 quart saucepan over high heat, cook 1 cup water, butter or margarine and salt until butter melts and mixture boils. Reduce heat to low; with wooden spoon, vigorously stir in flour until mixture forms a ball and leaves the side of the pan; remove from heat. Be careful not to overcook or drops of fat will form on the ball and paste will not puff. Let cook a minute or two.

Beat eggs into mixture until thoroughly blended. Continue beating until mixture is again very thick and smooth, and surface has a satin sheen.

Drop paste by ¼ cupful onto cookie sheet 2 inches apart and in rows 6 inches apart. With small spatula, spread each mound of paste into a 5 x ¾ inch rectangle, rounding edges. Traditionally, the chou paste is forced through a pastry bag.

Chou paste must be baked in a very hot oven so that it puffs immediately; continued baking firms the shell and makes it dry and lightweight. An underbaked shell will collapse when removed from the oven. Bake 4 minutes until lightly browned. To dry the inside, cut a slit in side of each shell to allow the steam to escape and bake 10 minutes longer. Cool shells on wire rack before filling. To fill shells, slice about ⅓ from the top of éach eclair shell and spoon in filling; replace tops and glaze

To make filling:

Prepare pudding mix as label directs but add almond extract. Cover surface with waxed paper. Refrigerate until chilled. Gently fold in whipped cream.

Chocolate Glaze:

In small saucepan over low heat, melt 2 squares semi-sweet chocolate and 2 tablespoons butter or margarine, stirring constantly. Stir in 1 cup confectioners' sugar and 3 tablespoons milk until smooth.

"SUPERB"

"RITZ" PECAN TORTE

Serves 4

3 egg whites

1/4 teaspoon cream of tartar

1 cup sugar

1/2 teaspoon vanilla

3/4 cup chopped pecans

20 Ritz crackers, finely crushed (Yes — Ritz!)

1/2 pint whipping cream

Preheat oven to 325°F. Beat egg whites and cream of tartar until stiff. Fold in sugar, vanilla, pecans and Ritz cracker crumbs.

Grease well 2 - 9 inch round cake tins; fill with egg white mixture. Bake for 30 minutes at 325°F. Cool for 15 minutes. Remove from tins.

Whip cream until stiff. Spread between two layers and refrigerate for 24 hours. Top with additional whipped cream.

(Believe me — this is delicious!)

Double for 8 servings.

MELON IN DAIQUIRI SAUCE

Serves 8

1 cantaloupe

1 small honeydew melon

1/4 watermelon

2/3 cup sugar

1/3 cup water

grated rind of 1 lime

juice of 2 limes

1/2 cup rum

1 or 2 cups fresh blueberries

fresh mint for garnish

Scoop melon balls from all the melons; refrigerate. In a saucepan, bring sugar and water to a boil. Reduce heat and simmer 5 minutes. Remove from heat; add lime rind; cool to room temperature. Stir in lime juice and rum. Pour sauce over fruit; add blueberries. Refrigerate 4 to 6 hours before serving.

Garnish with sprigs of fresh mint.

GRAND MARNIER SOUFFLÉ

Serves 8

4 egg yolks

1/2 cup sugar

3 tablespoons butter

3 tablespoons flour

1/4 teaspoon salt

1 cup scalded milk

4 egg whites

1 teaspoon vanilla

Grand Marnier, to taste (approximately 1/4 cup)

Butter and sugar a soufflé dish. Beat egg yolks with half the sugar until thick and lemon coloured.

Melt butter, stir in flour, salt and add hot milk gradually. Bring to boiling point and pour over egg yolks. Stir well and cool. Beat egg whites until stiff; add remaining sugar by spoonfuls. Fold into first mixture with vanilla and Grand Marnier. Bake in lower half of oven at 325°F for 40 minutes. Serve at once.

A very special ending to a meal.

COLD LEMON SOUFFLÉ

2 packages unflavoured gelatine

1/2 cup cold water

8 eggs, separated

2 cups sugar

3/4 cup lemon juice

1/2 teaspoon salt

1/4 cup Cointreau

2 to 3 teaspoons grated lemon rind

2 cups whipping cream

fresh berries

Wrap collar of foil around 6 cup soufflé dish, extending it 3 inches above dish. Butter collar lightly.

Sprinkle gelatine into water and let stand. Beat egg yolks, lemon juice, Cointreau, salt and 1 cup of sugar in top of double boiler. Cook 10 minutes, stirring constantly. Add gelatine and lemon rind. Remove from heat, pour into large bowl and chill until syrupy. Beat egg whites until stiff. Slowly add 1 cup of sugar. Whip cream until stiff. Fold egg whites and cream into egg yolk mixture quickly.

Pour in prepared souffle dish and chill 3 to 4 hours. Remove collar and serve with berries.

APPLE MOUSSE BRETONNE

Serves 6 to 8

4 or 5 tart medium-sized apples, peeled, cored and sliced

1/4 cup apricot preserve

1/2 teaspoon cinnamon

1/4 teaspoon freshly grated lemon peel

pinch of nutmeg

4 egg yolks

3/4 cup sugar

1 teaspoon cornstarch

1 1/2 cups milk, warmed

1 envelope gelatine

1 teaspoon vanilla

1 cup whipping cream

Apricot Sauce *

Combine apples, preserve, cinnamon, lemon peel and nutmeg in a large saucepan and cook over low heat until apples are very soft, stirring frequently to prevent scorching. Transfer mixture to blender or food processor and purée. Set aside.

Place yolks, sugar and cornstarch in top of double boiler and whisk until smooth. Add warm milk. Place mixture over simmering water and cook until thoroughly heated and slightly thickened, about 20 minutes stirring frequently. Add gelatine and vanilla; whisk until gelatine dissolves about 2 minutes. Transfer mixture to large bowl and chill until it just begins to set.

Whip cream and fold into chilled mixture. Add apple purée and whisk gently to blend. Taste and add more nutmeg and cinnamon if you wish. Pour into a 6 cup mould and chill.

Just before serving, unmould onto a plate. Spoon some Apricot Sauce around the mousse. Serve remaining sauce in sauce boat.

** Apricot Sauce*

1 cup apricot preserve

2 tablespoons lemon juice

2 tablespoons powdered sugar

1 teaspoon grated lemon peel

1/3 cup apricot brandy

Combine preserve, lemon juice, sugar and peel in small saucepan. Cook until preserves have melted and sugar is dissolved. Add apricot brandy. Sieve; then chill until just before serving.

JOHN J. ROBINETTE'S SWEDISH MERINGUE

Warning: This is a *very* high calorie recipe. It should be used only on special occasions and not more than twice a year. On other occasions eat fresh fruit and green salads.

Meringue:

4 egg whites

1 cup fruit sugar

1 cup ground *unblanched* almonds

Filling:

4 egg yolks

¾ cup fruit sugar

4 tablespoons cream

⅓ cup butter

2 tablespoons sherry

Topping:

½ pint whipping cream

Beat egg whites until almost stiff, add sugar gradually and beat until mixture forms stiff peaks. Fold in almonds. Bake in a well-greased large pie plate shaping up the sides. Bake in 325°F oven. Cool.

Beat egg yolks until light, with the sugar; add the cream and cook over hot water until thickened. (It will not be very thick). Add the butter and sherry. Stir, then cool. Put the filling in meringue and top with whipped cream. This should be done several hours before serving. You can even do it the day before but don't put the cream on until a few hours before serving.

CRÈME BRULÉE

Serves 6 to 8

3 cups heavy cream

6 tablespoons sugar

6 egg yolks

2 teaspoons vanilla

½ cup light brown sugar

6 or 8 ramekins (4 ounce oven-proof dishes)

Preheat oven to 300°F. In a double boiler heat cream over boiling water; add sugar. Stir until dissolved and very hot. In a bowl beat egg yolks until light; pour hot cream over yolks, beating vigorously. Stir in vanilla. Pour into individual ramekins. Set ramekins in pan of hot water about 1 inch deep, and place pan in oven. Bake at 300°F for 35 to 40 minutes. Cool; refrigerate until ice cold.

Sprinkle each ramekin lightly with brown sugar to cover surface. Place the ramekins in a pan with chipped ice. Slip the pan under the broiler and broil until sugar is melted and brown; about 1½ minutes. WATCH CAREFULLY. At this stage they can burn quickly. Chill again. May be done the day before.

For an added touch, serve with fresh strawberries.

ORANGE CHIFFON MOUSSE

Serves 8

1 envelope gelatine

¾ cup sugar

salt

2 eggs, separated

½ cup cold water

1-6 ounce can frozen unsweetened orange juice concentrate

1 cup heavy cream, whipped

In a saucepan, mix gelatine, ½ cup of sugar, and salt. In a small bowl, beat together egg yolks and water; stir this into gelatine mixture. Cook over medium heat and cook until gelatine dissolves and mixutre thickens slightly. Remove from heat; stir in frozen juice. Chill until mixture starts to set (about 45 minutes). Beat egg whites until stiff; add ¼ cup sugar and continue beating. Fold into orange mixture. Fold in whipped cream. Pour into a crystal bowl and chill. Decorate with whipped cream and orange curls.

An excellent light dessert after a heavy meal.

FROZEN LEMON DESSERT

Serves 8

6 eggs, separated

1 cup sugar

½ pint whipping cream

juice and rind of 2 lemons

½ cup graham cracker crumbs

Grease a spring-form pan. (Place a sheet of aluminum foil under pan in case of dripping during preparation.) Sprinkle two tablespoons of graham cracker crumbs on the bottom and sides of spring-form pan.

Beat 6 egg whites, with ½ cup sugar, until stiff. Beat egg yolks with ½ cup sugar until light and fluffy. Whip cream in a large bowl. Fold egg yolks into whipped cream; fold in egg whites. Fold in lemon juice and rind.

Alternate lemon mixture and graham cracker crumbs in spring-form pan. Freeze. Decorate with sliced lemon curls.

GÂTEAU GANACHE

Serves 8

Meringue:

6 egg whites

1 ½ cups sugar

¾ cup ground nuts (pecans or walnuts)

1 ½ teaspoons white wine vinegar

½ teaspoon vanilla

Parchment paper

Filling and Icing:

3 ounces semi-sweet chocolate

½ pint whipping cream

Place egg whites in a large mixing bowl and let stand an hour or so at room temperature.

Prepare two 8 inch cake tins as follows. Cut two rounds of parchment paper to fit bottom of pans. Grease and lightly flour cake tin bottoms and sides, cover bottom with fitted paper, grease and lightly flour paper. Beat egg whites until stiff. Add sugar and nuts all at once and fold in gently with a metal spoon. Add vinegar and vanilla and spoon lightly into prepared tins. Bake at 375°F for 35 to 40 minutes (or until crusty to the touch). Turn onto racks immediately and peel off parchment. (This can all be done the day before.)

Melt chocolate in double boiler and cool. Whip cream until very stiff. Put half of cream in a separate bowl and add half to the chocolate. Place one meringue round on serving platter and cover with this mixture. Top with second meringue. Cover second meringue with balance of whipped cream. Dip spatula into melted chocolate and make swirls on the whipped cream so that it has marbled effect. Use *plenty* of chocolate. Store dessert in refrigerator until ready to serve.

LEMON SPONGE

Serves 4

3 egg yolks

1 cup sugar

2 tablespoons melted butter

1 cup milk

3 tablespoons flour

1 lemon (juice and grated rind)

3 egg whites

Beat egg yolks, add sugar, melted butter, milk, flour, lemon rind and juice. Cut and fold in beaten egg whites.

Place dish in pan of 1 inch hot water. Bake at 350°F for 45 minutes.

GRANDMOTHER'S CREAM CHEESE SOVAS

Serves 6

2 tablespoons unflavoured gelatine

1 cup cold water

1-16 ounce package cream cheese, softened

2 tablespoons orange rind, grated

¾ teaspoon salt

½ cup undiluted orange juice

1 cup peach juice

1-19 ounce can peach halves, drained

In a saucepan sprinkle gelatine onto cold water and let stand for 5 minutes. Dissolve over hot water. Add cream cheese and mix well before adding rind, salt, orange and peach juice.

Pour into wet moulds and chill. Unmould and serve with peach halves.

REFRIGERATED CHEESE CAKE *Serves 8*

Crust:

1 cup crushed graham wafers

3 tablespoons sugar

1 teaspoon cinnamon

3 tablespoons melted butter

Mix all together and press into a 9 inch pie plate and chill.

Filling:

1 envelope gelatine

1/4 cup cold water

2 egg yolks

1/2 cup white sugar

1 tablespoon milk

3/4 pound cream cheese (1 1/2 - 8 ounce packages)

1 tablespoon lemon juice

rind of 1 lemon

1 teaspoon vanilla

2 egg whites

1 cup 35% cream, whipped.

Dissolve the gelatine in water and let stand. Beat the egg yolks in the top of a double boiler; add the sugar and milk; mix well and cook until thick, stirring often. Remove from the heat and add the gelatine, stirring, until dissolved.

In a large bowl, cream the cheese, removing any lumps, and gradually add the gelatine mixture. Add the lemon juice, rind, and vanilla. In another bowl, beat the egg whites until stiff, and carefully fold into mixture with the whipped cream.

Pour into crumb-lined pan and refrigerate for 6 to 8 hours.

Topping:

1-15 ounce can red pitted cherries

1/3 cup sugar

2 tablespoons cornstarch

1 teaspoon red food colouring

Drain cherries, reserving the juice. In a saucepan, add enough water to the cherry juice to make 1 cup. Bring to a rolling boil.

Combine the sugar and cornstarch and add a little of the hot liquid to make a paste. Reduce the heat of the juice and add the paste to it, stirring constantly until it becomes slightly thick and transparent. Remove from heat, add colouring and carefully fold in cherries. Cool slightly before pouring over cheesecake.

N.B. To double — recipe must be made twice.

CHOCOLATE MARSHMALLOW DESSERT

Serves 8 to 10

1 tablespoon unflavoured gelatine

1/4 cup cold water

1/2 cup coca

2 cups milk (or 1 cup strong coffee and 1 cup milk)

1 pound marshmallows

4 egg yolks slightly beaten

1/2 teaspoon salt

1 teaspoon vanilla

1/2 cup whipping cream, whipped

1/4 cup sugar

4 egg whites

14 ladyfingers (or strips of sponge cake)

Soak gelatine in cold water for 5 minutes. In a heavy saucepan, combine cocoa, milk and whole marshmallows. Over low heat stir constantly until cocoa is blended and marshmallows are completely dissolved. Remove from heat: stir until marshmallows are completely dissolved.Slowly add egg yolks. Return to heat and stirring constantly, cook until mixture begins to thicken, i.e., coats spoon.

Add gelatine, salt and flavouring. Chill *somewhat.*

Fold in whipped cream and egg whites stiffly beaten with sugar. Line mould with ladyfingers and pour in beaten mixture.

GERMAN ALMOND TORTE

Serves 6 to 8

4 eggs, separated
1 cup icing sugar
1/2 cup chopped almonds
1 teaspoon baking powder
3/4 cup finely crushed cracker crumbs
raspberry jam
1/2 pint whipping cream

Beat egg yolks until thick. Gradually add sugar. Fold in egg whites, beaten until stiff. Add almonds, baking powder and cracker crumbs.

Bake in a slow oven 275°F for 1 hour. It will be tough if cooked too fast. Cool. Split and spread with jam.

Put together and cover with sweetened whipped cream.

COFFEE CREAM

Serves 6 to 8

1 1/2 cups strong coffee
1/2 cup milk
2/3 cup of sugar
1 tablespoon gelatine
1/2 teaspoon salt
3 eggs, separated
1/2 teaspoon vanilla

Mix coffee, milk, half the sugar; add the gelatine and heat in a double boiler until the gelatine is dissolved. Add remaining sugar and salt. Add the egg yolks, slightly beaten. Cook mixture, stirring constantly, until mixture coats the spoon. Remove from heat, cool slightly.

Beat egg whites until stiff; fold into the cooled egg yolk mixture and add vanilla. Mould and chill. Serve with whipped cream.

This is very attractive in a glass bowl.

COFFEE TORTONI

Serves 10

3 egg whites

¾ cup sugar

3 teaspoons finely powdered instant coffee

1½ cups whipping cream

1 teaspoon vanilla or rum

½ cup toasted almonds

Beat egg whites until frothy. Beat in sugar about 1 tablespoon at a time. Add coffee powder and beat until stiff and "satiny".

In separate bowl, whip cream with vanilla or rum until thick, but still frothy. Fold into egg white mixture and add toasted almonds.

Put in serving dish and freeze overnight or longer if you wish.

FIVE LAYER BLUEBERRY TART

Serves 16

Layer 1:

2 cups graham cracker crumbs

½ cup melted butter

Blend together and press into a 9 inch x 13 inch pan. Bake 15 minutes at 300°F then cool.

Layer 2:

½ cup soft butter, creamed

1½ cups icing sugar

2 eggs

Cream icing sugar and butter; beat in eggs until light. Spread over first layer.

Layer 3:

Spread 1-19 ounce can blueberry pie filling over layer 2.

Layer 4:

1-19 ounce can crushed pineapple (drained)

1 cup Cool Whip

Fold together and spread over layer 3.

Layer 5:

Sprinkle ½ cup graham cracker crumbs over entire top of layer 4.

Let stand in refrigerator for 2 hours, or overnight, which gives the best results.

CYNTHIA WINE'S ORANGES IN WINE

Serves 6

1 cup dry red wine

1 cup water

1/3 cup honey

2 cinnamon sticks

2 cloves

2 slices of lemon

6 large oranges

1/2 pint whipped cream

Combine wine, water, honey, cinnamon, cloves and lemon. Bring to a boil; simmer three minutes. Remove cloves and keep the syrup hot.

Meanwhile, peel oranges and reserve skins. Section oranges, keeping the segments as whole as possible. Discard the fibrous membranes. Drop orange sections into the hot syrup.

Pare away white part of orange skins and cut skins into very fine julienne strips. Sprinkle the strips over oranges in red wine; chill. Serve with sweetened whipped cream.

CARAMEL FLAN

Serves 6

2 ¾ cups scalded milk

rind of ½ orange, grated

1 cinnamon stick

4 eggs

4 egg yolks

¼ cup dark rum

¾ cup sugar

Caramel:

¾ cup sugar

⅓ cup water

Make the caramel by heating the sugar in water until it dissolves. Bring the mixture to a boil and boil until it turns a deep gold colour. Remove from heat and pour into 1 ½ quart baking dish, covering the whole bottom of dish. Cool.

Beat all the remaining ingredients together and pour into baking dish. Set baking dish into another dish partially filled with hot water. Bake at 350°F for 1 ½ hours.

Serve warm. Loosen with a knife and turn out onto a shallow serving dish.

SOUFFLÉ ELVA

Serves 12

2 envelopes gelatine

1 ½ cups strong coffee (hot)

½ cup Tia Maria, or any coffee liqueur

6 eggs, separated

1 cup white sugar

4 teaspoons lemon juice

1 cup whipping cream

Dissolve gelatine in hot coffee; add Tia Maria. Let stand until consistency of an unbeaten egg white. Beat egg whites until stiff; add ½ cup sugar. Beat in lemon juice. Beat egg yolks until light and fluffy; add ½ cup sugar. Beat well. Whip cream until it forms soft peaks.

Beat gelatine mixture into egg yolks (be sure to beat it very thoroughly). Fold the egg yolk mixture into egg whites; then fold this mixture into whipped cream until no white blobs of cream show.

Pour into large bowl, and chill. Decorate with whipped cream rosettes flavored with a little Tia Maria and shavings of semi-sweet chocolate when serving.

PARTY TORTE

Serves 8

Make the day before.

8 egg whites

1 1/2 teaspoons vanilla

1 teaspoon vinegar

2 cups sifted sugar

Beat egg whites with vinegar to form peaks; add vanilla and add sugar 1 tablespoon at a time to make meringue. Spread gently in two 9 inch layer cake pans, lined with heavy brown or waxed paper. Bake in a slow 300°F oven for 1 1/4 hours. Cool well in pans and turn onto serving plate.

Filling:

1 cup crushed pineapple, well drained

3/4 cup maraschino cherries, drained and cut in quarters

2 cups heavy cream, whipped

Fold fruit into cream and spread generously over one meringue. Top with second meringue. Frost with remainder of filling. Chill overnight.

NUT REFRIGERATOR CAKE

Serves 15

30 macaroons

18 ladyfingers

1 1/3 cups icing sugar

1 cup butter

3 eggs

3 eggs, separated

1/2 pound blanched almonds, or pecans, cut in half

1 teaspoon vanilla

salt

1/2 pint whipping cream

nuts or cherries for garnish

Line bottom and sides of a dish, first with waxed paper, then with ladyfingers, and then with a layer of macaroons. Cream butter and icing sugar, add 3 eggs, one at a time, beating well after each addition. Add three well-beaten egg yolks with vanilla, salt and nuts. Fold in stiffly beaten egg whites.

Pour half the mixture over macaroons, add another layer of macaroons, then the remaining half of the mixture. Refrigerate for 30 hours. Cover with whipped cream and nuts or cherries.

LONDON PUDDING

Serves 10 to 12

½ pound butter

½ cup icing sugar

1 egg, well beaten

¼ teaspoon vanilla

2 tablespoons cold strong coffee

2 packages ladyfingers

toasted sliced almonds

Cream together butter and sugar. Add beaten egg and vanilla. In loaf pan place a layer of halved ladyfingers, sprinkle with some coffee and spread with some butter mixture. Keep repeating until dessert fills pan. Chill until firm or overnight.

Invert on plate and ice dessert with remaining butter mixture. Sprinkle with toasted almonds.

TRIFLE

Serves 8

2½ cups milk

6 eggs

¼ cup sugar

1 teaspoon vanilla

2 packages ladyfingers

sherry

3 to 4 tablespoons jam or jelly (seedless raspberry jam is very nice)

toasted slivered almonds, browned in a little butter

½ pint whipping cream

Custard, make the day before:

Scald milk; beat eggs with sugar. Add milk slowly to beaten eggs and cook over boiling water until thick. Add vanilla and cool. Chill in refrigerator overnight. Custard should be quite thick.

Next day, line the bottom of a pretty glass bowl with a layer of ladyfingers. Sprinkle generously with sherry. Dab with jam. Cover with part of custard. Sprinkle with almonds. Repeat layers until bowl is almost filled. Cover with whipped cream, top with remaining almonds. Chill well.

A treat to behold.

NUBIAN CHOCOLATE ROLL

Serves 6 to 8

6 eggs, separated

3/4 cup granulated sugar

1/3 cup unsweetened cocoa

1 teaspoon vanilla extract

1 teaspoon cinnamon

1/2 teaspoon ground anise

confectioners' sugar

Filling:

1 1/2 cups heavy cream

1/3 cup confectioners' sugar

3 tablespoons unsweetened cocoa

1 teaspoon vanilla extract

pistachios or walnuts, chopped

In large bowl of electric mixer, let egg whites stand 1 hour. Preheat oven to 375°F. Lightly grease bottom of 15 1/2 x 10 1/2 x 1 inch jelly roll pan; line with oiled waxed paper.

At high speed, beat whites until soft peaks form. Gradually beat in 1/4 cup granulated sugar, beating until stiff. Using same beaters, at high speed, beat yolks with remainder of granulated sugar, until thick and lemon coloured. Stir in flavourings. With wire whisk or rubber scraper and using an under and over motion, gently fold yolk mixture into egg whites. Spread evenly in prepared pan. Bake 12 minutes, until surface springs back when pressed with finger.

Onto a clean towel sift confectioners' sugar in 15 x 10 inch rectangle. Turn out cake onto sugar; peel off paper. With knife, trim edges. From long side, roll up cake in towel, jelly-roll fashion. Cool on rack, seam side down.

Make filling. In medium bowl, combine cream, sugar, cocoa, and vanilla. Refrigerate 1 hour. Beat until stiff. Gently unroll cake; remove towel. Spread with three fourths filling; reroll. Spread with rest of filling; sprinkle with nuts. Place seam side down. Refrigerate.

This cake is worth the effort.

LIME ICE

Serves 8

1 1/3 cups sugar

4 cups cold water

1 cup lime juice

a few drops of green food colouring

Heat the sugar with the water over low heat until dissolved. Bring to a boil and simmer for 8 minutes. Cool.

Add the lime juice and colouring; taste for sweetness. Chill. Freeze the mixture in a churn freezer. Cover tightly and store in the freezer.

BISCUIT TORTONI

Serves 12

3 egg whites

1/4 cup water

3/4 cup sugar

dash salt

4 cups whole blanched almonds

almond extract

1 1/2 cups heavy cream

3/4 teaspoons vanilla extract

12 candied cherries

In small bowl, let egg whites warm to room temperature, about 1 hour. Combine 1/4 cup water with sugar in a 1 quart saucepan, cook over low heat, stirring, until sugar is dissolved. Bring to boiling over medium heat; boil uncovered and without stirring to 236°F on candy thermometer, or until syrup spins a 2 inch thread when dropped from a spoon.

Meanwhile, at high speed, beat egg whites with salt just until stiff peaks form when beater is slowly raised. Pour hot syrup in a thin stream over egg whites, beating constantly until mixture forms very stiff peaks when beater is raised. Refrigerate covered for 30 minutes.

Preheat oven to 350°F. Place almonds in shallow pan and bake until toasted 8 to 10 minutes. Finely grind almonds in a blender. Turn into small bowl. Blend in 1 1/2 teaspoon almond extract and set aside.

In medium bowl beat cream with 1/4 teaspoon almond extract and the vanilla until stiff. With wire whisk or rubber scraper fold into egg white mixture until thoroughly combined.

Spoon into 12 paper lined 2 1/2 inch muffin pan cups, sprinkle with almond mixture, top with a cherry. Cover with foil, freeze until firm or overnight. Serve directly from freezer.

Baking

FOREST RANGERS

Makes 2 dozen Cookies

1 cup white sugar

1 cup brown sugar

1 cup butter

2 eggs

2 cups of quick oats

2 cups of Rice Krispies

2 cups of coconut

2 cups of flour

1 teaspoon baking soda

½ teaspoon baking powder

1 teaspoon vanilla

In a large bowl cream butter and sugars; beat in eggs. Mix together oats, Rice Krispies and coconut. Sift together flour, baking powder and baking soda; add to cereal mixture. Stir in vanilla, add butter and sugar mixture.

Drop by spoonful onto a greased cookie sheet.

Bake at 350°F for 12 to 15 minutes, or until golden.

DAD'S COOKIE BARS

Makes 24 Bars

24 crushed "Dad's" oatmeal cookies

½ cup melted butter

2 squares semi-sweet chocolate

1 square bitter chocolate

½ cup butter

1 egg

1 teaspoon vanilla

1½ cups icing sugar

Blend melted butter and cookies and press ⅔ of mixture in 8 x 8 inch pan lined with wax paper. Bake at 350°F for 5 minutes.

Melt chocolate and butter in double boiler. Remove from heat and beat in egg, vanilla and icing sugar.

Pour over cookie crust, top with remaining crumbs and refrigerate.

FROSTED DATE BALLS

Makes 36 Balls

½ cup butter

⅓ cup powdered sugar

1 tablespoon milk

1 teaspoon vanilla

1 ¼ cups flour

¼ teaspoon salt

⅔ cup chopped dates

½ cup chopped nuts

Cream butter and sugar. Add milk and vanilla. Stir in flour and salt, then blend in dates and nuts. Roll in 1 inch balls; place 3 inches apart on ungreased baking sheet.

Bake in 300°F oven about 20 minutes; until light brown. While still warm, roll in powdered sugar.

PEANUT WHEAT CRUNCHIES

Makes 3 dozen Crunchies

½ cup peanut butter

½ cup butter

1 cup brown sugar

1 egg

1 ½ teaspoons vanilla

1 cup whole wheat flour

¾ teaspoon salt

¼ teaspoon baking powder

¼ teaspoon baking soda

1 cup large flake oats

1 cup coarsely chopped salted peanuts

¾ cup raisins (optional)

Cream butters together. Beat in sugar, egg, and vanilla. Blend the flour with salt, baking powder and soda. Stir into butter mixture. Stir in remaining ingredients.

Form into small balls and place on greased cookie sheet. Flatten slightly with floured fork. Bake at 375°F for 8 minutes or until they start to brown. Watch closely. Cool on pan for 2 minutes. Remove to rack.

CURLED WAFERS

Makes 2 dozen Wafers

2 egg whites

½ cup fruit sugar

1 ¼ cups flour

¼ cup butter, melted and cooled

1 teaspoon rum, or almond flavouring

1 teaspoon coarsely grated orange rind

½ cup toasted almond slices, optional

Beat egg whites and sugar until white and stiff. Add flour, butter, flavouring, rind and nuts to mixture.

Drop ½ teaspoons of batter, well spaced, on buttered cookie sheet. Bake at 350°F for 5 to 6 minutes.

Remove from sheet and place over a rolling pin until cool and curled.

CHINESE CHEWS

Makes 16 Squares

1 cup sugar

¼ cup melted butter

2 eggs

2 tablespoons milk

1 teaspoon vanilla

1 cup flour

1 teaspoon baking powder

1 cup chopped walnuts

1 cup chopped dates

Mix sugar, butter, eggs, milk and vanilla. Beat well. Mix in flour with salt, baking powder, and blend well. Add dates and nuts. Spread in greased 8 x 8 inch cake pan and bake at 375°F for 20 minutes.

HAGOOD HARDY'S FAVOURITE AFTER-DINNER TREAT – CHOCOLATE BALLS

2 cups sifted icing sugar

1 cup flaked coconut

1 cup chopped walnuts

¼ cup soft butter

¼ cup evaporated milk

4 squares unsweetened chocolate

8 squares semi-sweetened chocolate

1 square inch paraffin wax

Mix together icing sugar, coconut, walnuts and butter. Stir in evaporated milk. Cover and chill for one hour.

Roll into little balls (about the size of a cherry tomato). Chill again for one hour.

In a double boiler, melt together, chocolate squares and paraffin wax and allow to cool. Using a toothpick, dip the balls into the chocolate mixture to coat. Place on wax paper and chill.

DELICIOUS!!!

KID'S FAVOURITES

Makes 2 dozen Cookies

1-6 ounce package chocolate chips

1-6 ounce package butterscotch chips

1-6 ounce package shelled peanuts

1-4 ounce can Chinese noodles

Melt all the chips together. Stir in the peanuts and Chinese noodles. Drop by spoonful onto cookie sheet covered with waxed paper. Cool. Store in refrigerator or they freeze beautifully.

ORANGE SQUARES

Makes 8 Squares

1/3 cup butter

1 cup sifted all-purpose flour

1 tablespoon orange rind

1 tablespoon sugar

2 eggs

2 tablespoons flour

1/2 teaspoon baking powder

1 1/2 cups brown sugar

1/4 teaspoon salt

1/2 cup coconut

Blend together first four ingredients until crumbly. Press into 9 inch cake pan and bake 10 minutes at 350°F. Set aside.

Beat eggs and blend in dry ingredients. Stir in coconut and pour over baked layer. Bake 25 to 30 minutes at 350°F. Cool, ice and cut into squares.

ORANGE BUTTER ICING

2 tablespoons soft butter

1 egg yolk

2 teaspoons grated orange rind

1 tablespoon orange juice

Blend butter, yolk, sugar and orange rind. Add juice carefully until desired spreading consistency is achieved.

A perfect companion for coffee — after a meeting?

BRANDY BALLS

Makes 36 to 42

2 cups vanilla wafer crumbs

2 tablespoons cocoa

1 1/2 cups confectioners' sugar, divided

1 cup pecans, very finely chopped

2 tablespoons white corn syrup

1/4 cup brandy

Thoroughly mix the vanilla wafer crumbs, cocoa, pecans and 1 cup confectioners' sugar. Add the corn syrup and brandy, mix well.

Shape into 1 inch balls and roll into remaining confectioners' sugar. Put in a tightly covered tin box or other metal container for at least 12 hours before serving.

Note: These cookies keep well for 4 or 5 weeks.

DOUBLE-DECK BROWNIES

Makes 15 to 20 Squares

2/3 cup sifted all-purpose flour

1/2 teaspoon baking powder

1/4 teaspoon salt

2 eggs

1 cup granulated sugar

1/3 cup melted butter or shortening

1/3 cup flaked coconut

1/2 teaspoon almond extract

1 1/2 squares unsweetened chocolate, melted

Sift flour with baking powder and salt. Beat eggs well, gradually adding sugar. Stir in melted butter; blend in flour mixture, mix thoroughly.

Into small bowl pour 1/4 of batter. Stir in coconut and almond extract. Into remaining batter blend melted chocolate. Spread chocolate batter evenly in 8 x 8 x 2 inch pan.

Drop almond coconut batter by spoonful on chocolate mixture and then spread evenly, carefully, with knife or spatula. Bake at 350°F for 35 minutes or until very light golden colour.

Cool slightly. Cut in squares.

BUTTERSCOTCH BROWNIES

Makes approximately 16 Brownies

1/4 cup butter

1 cup brown sugar

1 egg

1 teaspoon vanilla

1/2 cup sifted all-purpose flour

1 teaspoon baking powder

1/2 teaspoon salt

3/4 cup finely chopped nuts

In a saucepan melt butter; stir in brown sugar, until sugar is dissolved.

Cool slightly.

Beat in vigorously, egg and vanilla. Sift together the flour and baking powder. Stir dry ingredients into butter mixture; add nuts.

Pour the batter into a greased 9 x 9 inch pan. Bake at 350°F for 20 to 25 minutes. Cool and cut.

HEALTH LOAF

1/2 cup boiling water

1/2 cup raisins

1 beaten egg

1/4 cup brown sugar

1 cup natural bran

1 cup quick rolled oats

1 cup whole wheat flour

1/4 cup raw wheat germ

2 teaspoons baking soda

1/2 teaspoon salt

1 cup buttermilk (or skim milk soured with lemon juice)

Pour boiling water over raisins; cool.

In a large bowl, blend egg and sugar. Stir together bran, oats, flour, wheat germ, soda and salt. Add to egg and sugar, with buttermilk, cooled raisins and water. Stir to blend thoroughly.

Pour into greased 9 x 5 x 3 inch pan. Bake at 350°F for 45 minutes or until wooden pick inserted in centre comes out clean.

Cool and keep in refrigerator.

Suitable for diabetics. Loaf will cut into 25 slices. 1 slice equals 1 starch.

CHEESE DROP BISCUITS *Makes 1 dozen Biscuits*

1 cup sharp Cheddar cheese

1 cup all-purpose flour

1/4 cup butter

2 teaspoons baking powder

1/2 cup very cold water

In food processor, grate 1 cup sharp Cheddar cheese. Remove; put in steel blade. Add: flour, butter and baking powder; mix. Add cheese and water; mix until consistency of dough.

Drop biscuits onto cookie sheet. Bake at 400°F for 8 to 10 minutes.

LEMON BREAD *Makes 1 loaf*

1/2 cup shortening

1 cup sugar

2 eggs

1/2 cup milk

1 1/2 cups flour

1/2 teaspoon salt

1 teaspoon baking powder

1/4 cup chopped nuts

grated rind and juice of 1 lemon) } glaze

1/4 sugar } glaze

Cream shortening; add sugar. Mix in eggs. Add dry ingredients alternately with milk. Add nuts and lemon rind.

Pour into greased 9 x 5 x 3 inch loaf pan. Bake at 350°F for 55 minutes.

Remove from oven. Pierce top of loaf 15 to 20 times with a skewer.

Gently pour over the loaf the dissolved solution of lemon juice and 1/4 cup sugar. Let stand for 20 minutes before removing from pan.

This lemon bread freezes well.

STRAWBERRY BREAD

Makes 2 Loaves

3 cups flour

1 teaspoon baking soda

1 teaspoon salt

1 teaspoon cinnamon

2 cups sugar

4 eggs, well beaten

½ cup salad oil

1 teaspoon vanilla

⅔ cups chopped nuts

2 cups (16 ounce package) frozen strawberries, thawed

Blend in order given; pour into two greased and floured loaf pans. Bake at 350°F for 40 to 50 minutes.

COFFEE CAN BREAD

1 package dry yeast

½ cup warm water

1 cup milk

2 tablespoons margarine

2 tablespoons honey

1 teaspoon salt

1 egg, beaten

1 cup corn meal

1¾ cups flour

1¾ cups flour

Dissolve yeast in warm water. In a saucepan, scald milk; add butter. Cool to lukewarm; stir in honey, salt, egg and cornmeal. Blend with mixer on low speed. Add 1¾ cups flour. Stir with wooden spoon. Then, add 1¾ cups flour. Mix well.

Place dough in a well-buttered 2 pound coffee can; grease the plastic cover as well and cover can. Set in a warm place to rise. The cover will pop off when ready to bake.

Bake at 350°F for 1¼ hours. Cool in can for 10 minutes, remove carefully and cool loaf upright.

Note: 2 - 1 pound cans may be used for smaller loaves

COTTAGE CHEESE PANCAKES

Serves 4

6 eggs

1 1/2 cups cottage cheese

1/2 teaspoon salt

1/2 cup flour

Beat eggs until light.

Mash cheese or beat in electric mixer or with rotary beater until almost smooth. Add to eggs with salt and flour; mix thoroughly.

Cook like ordinary pancakes.

1/2 recipe "pour deux".

DILLED CASSEROLE BREAD

Serves 10

1 package dry yeast

1/4 cup warm water

1 cup creamed cottage cheese

2 tablespoons sugar

1 tablespoon onion, minced

1 tablespoon butter

2 teaspoons dill seed

1 teaspoon salt

1/4 teaspoon soda

1 egg, unbeaten

2 1/2 cups all-purpose flour

melted butter

In a saucepan, heat cottage cheese to lukewarm. Soften yeast in water. In a large mixing bowl combine cottage cheese, sugar, onion, butter, dill seed, salt, soda, egg and softened yeast. Add flour to make a stiff dough, beating well after each addition. Cover. Let rise in a warm place, when doubled in size (approximately 60 minutes) punch down dough. Turn into a well-greased 8 inch round 2 quart casserole dish. Let rise again in a warm place (approximately 40 minutes). Bake at 350°F for 30 to 40 minutes. Brush with melted butter. Serve warm.

This bread freezes beautifully.

HELLO DOLLY'S

Makes approximately 32 Squares

½ cup butter

1 cup crushed graham crackers

1 cup coconut

1-6 ounce package chocolate chips

1-6 ounce package butterscotch chips

1 cup chopped walnuts

1 cup condensed milk

Melt butter, add graham crackers, mix well, press into 9 x 13 inch cake pan.
Combine all other ingredients, and spread on graham cracker base. Bake at 350°F for 30 minutes. Cool and cut in squares.

WALNUT CRESCENTS

Makes approximately 30 Cookies

1 cup soft butter

¼ cup icing sugar

2 teaspoons vanilla

1¾ cups all-purpose flour

1 cup finely chopped walnuts

icing sugar

Cream butter, add sugar, vanilla and mix well. Blend in flour and nuts.
Shape dough into small rolls, ½ inch in diameter and 1 inch long. Bend slightly to make a crescent shape.
Bake at 375°F about 15 minutes. Cool slightly and roll in icing sugar. Cool completely and roll in sugar again before storing.

MERINGUE CHOCOLATE CHIP COOKIES

Makes about 20 Cookies

2 egg whites, stiffly beaten

¼ teaspoon salt

¼ teaspoon cream of tartar

¾ cup sugar

½ teaspoon vanilla

1-6 ounce package chocolate chips

Add salt, cream of tartar, sugar and vanilla to stiffly beaten egg whites. Fold in chocolate chips. Line a cookie sheet with ungreased heavy paper. Drop mixture by teaspoonful on the paper.
Bake at 300°F for 25 minutes.

6

Florentines
Recipe on page 194

Hello Dolly's
Recipe on page 192

Meringue Chocolate Chip Cookies
Recipe on page 192

Peanut Butter Squares
Recipe on page 193

Scandinavian Thumb Cookies
Recipe on page 194

Toffee Squares
Recipe on page 193

Vanessa C. Harwood's Nanaimo Bars
Recipe on page 195

Walnut Crescents
Recipe on page 192

TOFFEE SQUARES

Makes 20 Squares

1 cup butter

1 cup brown sugar

2 cups flour

1 egg yolk, beaten

1 teaspoon vanilla

1-18 ounce bar sweet chocolate

1 cup walnuts, chopped

Cream butter and sugar. Add beaten egg yolk, vanilla and flour. Spread thinly on cookie sheet. Bake at 350°F for 20 minutes.

Melt chocolate bar in top of double boiler; spread on cookie base while warm. Sprinkle with nuts and cut in squares while warm.

PEANUT BUTTER SQUARES

Makes 16 Squares

½ cup corn syrup

½ cup brown sugar

1 cup chunky peanut butter

2 cups corn flakes

1 cup Rice Krispies

Cook syrup and sugar over medium heat until boiling. Remove from heat, add peanut butter, corn flakes and Rice Krispies. Stir well and press into greased 9 x 9 inch pan.

Icing:

1 cup brown sugar

2 tablespoons butter

3 tablespoons cream

1 cup icing sugar

Combine brown sugar, butter and cream in saucepan; bring to boil over medium heat. Boil for one minute. Add up to 1 cup of icing sugar to thicken. Spread icing over crispy mixture, and chill. *Store in refrigerator.*

SCANDINAVIAN THUMB COOKIES

Makes 24 Cookies

½ cup butter

¼ cup brown sugar

1 egg, separated

1 cup flour

½ cup chopped nuts

red currant jelly

Cream butter and sugar. Add egg yolk and beat until light. Blend in flour and roll dough in 1 inch balls. Dip balls in egg white and roll in nuts.

Put on cookie sheet and make a depression in each ball with your thumb. Bake 3 minutes in a *slow oven* at 300°F. Remove and press down depression again. Continue baking 15 minutes longer. Cool. Fill centres with jelly.

Pretty on a Plate and Good to Eat.

FLORENTINES

Makes 24 Cookies

⅓ cup candied cherries

⅔ cup mixed peel

¼ cup raisins

⅓ cup blanched almonds

½ cup sifted all-purpose flour

¼ cup butter

¼ cup sugar

1 tablespoon light corn syrup

1 tablespoon lemon juice

2 squares semi-sweet OR bitter chocolate

Chop cherries, peel, raisins and almonds finely and dredge in flour.

Melt butter and add sugar, syrup and lemon juice. Stir fruit and flour mixture into melted butter mixture.

Drop batter by teaspoonful onto greased baking sheet, well spaced. Flatten with the bottom of a wet tumbler. Bake 8 to 10 minutes in 350°F oven until they have stopped sizzling and are a deep golden brown with lacy edges. Let them stand for a minute before lifting them with a spatula and placing on a wire rack. Melt chocolate over hot water and frost the flat undersides of the cookies. They freeze very well.

VANESSA C. HARWOOD'S NANAIMO BARS

Makes 2 dozen Bars

½ cup butter or margarine

5 tablespoons cocoa

1 teaspoon vanilla

¼ cup white sugar

1 egg

2 cups graham wafer crumbs

1 cup flaked coconut

½ cup chopped walnuts

¼ cup butter

2 tablespoons custard powder

2 cups icing sugar

2 to 3 tablespoons milk

3 squares semi-sweet chocolate

1 tablespoon butter

Mix ½ cup butter, cocoa, white sugar, egg and vanilla. Set over boiling water and stir until mixture resembles a custard. Add crumbs, coconut and nuts. Press into 8 inch square pan.

Cream ¼ cup butter, custard powder, icing sugar and milk. Spread icing over mixture in pan.

Melt chocolate and butter over hot water and spread over icing. Chill and cut into bars.

HEARTY COOKIES

Makes 3 dozen Cookies

1 cup margarine

3 cups quick-cooking rolled oats

1 cup granulated sugar

¾ cup all-purpose flour

1 teaspoon baking soda

½ teaspoon ground cloves

½ teaspoon cinnamon

½ cup dried currants

¼ cup milk

Preheat oven to 350°F and grease cookie sheets. Cream margarine with sugar. Blend in rolled oats.

Sift together dry ingredients and add to above mixture. Add currants and mix in milk.

Drop by teaspoonful onto cookie sheet and flatten with floured fork. Bake 10 to 15 minutes.

HERMITS

Makes 3 dozen Cookies

3 cups of flour, sifted

1 teaspoon baking soda

½ teaspoon nutmeg

½ teaspoon cinnamon

½ teaspoon salt

1½ cups chopped nuts

¼ cup chopped mixed peel

1 cup raisins

1 cup currants

½ cup butter or margarine

1½ cups brown sugar

2 eggs

2 tablespoons sour milk

Sift together flour, soda and spices. In another bowl, place all fruits and nuts. Sprinkle some of the flour mixture over the fruits to separate them. Cream butter and sugar, beat in eggs and sour milk. Add flour and fruits to the creamed mixture.

Drop by teaspoonful onto a greased cookie sheet and bake at 350°F for 15 minutes.

CINDY NICHOLAS' BANANA ALL-BRAN MUFFINS

Makes 9 Muffins

1 cup All-Bran

1/2 cup milk

1 egg

1/4 cup shortening, melted

3 or 4 bananas, sliced

1 cup sifted all-purpose flour

1/4 cup sugar

2 1/2 teaspoons baking powder

1/2 teaspoon salt

1/2 teaspoon cinnamon

1. Combine All-Bran and milk. Let stand until most of moisture is absorbed. Add egg, shortening and bananas. Beat well.
2. Sift together flour, sugar, baking powder, salt and cinnamon. Add to bran mixture, stirring well. Fill greased muffin cups full.
3. Bake at 400°F for 20 to 25 minutes.

SPICED PUMPKIN MUFFINS

Makes 10 medium-sized Muffins

1/3 cup shortening

1/2 cup packed brown sugar

1 egg

1/2 cup canned or mashed cooked pumpkin

1 1/2 cups sifted flour

3 teaspoons baking powder

1/2 teaspoon salt

1/2 teaspoon each cinnamon and nutmeg

1/4 teaspoon ginger

3/4 cup milk

Cream together shortening and sugar until light. Add egg and again beat. Add pumpkin and mix. Sift dry ingredients together. Add to sugar mixture alternately with milk, beating well after each addition.

Fill greased muffin tins 2/3 full with batter. Bake at 375°F for 25 minutes.

PUMPKIN BREAD

Makes 2 Loaves

1 1/2 cups sugar

1/2 cup salad oil

2 eggs

1 cup cooked pumpkin

1 2/3 cups flour

1 1/4 teaspoons baking powder

1/4 teaspoon baking soda

3/4 teaspoon salt

1/2 teaspoon cloves

1/2 teaspoon cinnamon

1/2 teaspoon nutmeg

nuts, if desired, (pecans, walnuts)

Mix sugar, oil, eggs and pumpkin. Mix dry ingredients together, add to pumpkin mixture. Stir in nuts.

Bake in 2 small, greased loaf pans at 325°F for 1 to 1 1/2 hours.

JOAN SUTTON'S BUTTERSCOTCH BANANA STICKY BUNS

Makes 12 Buns

¾ cup ripe bananas, mashed

2 cups Bisquick

2 tablespoons butter, softened

¼ cup brown sugar

½ cup brown sugar

½ cup butter, melted

pecan halves

Preheat oven to 450°F.

In a bowl, add bananas to Bisquick and mix thoroughly with a fork. On a board, lightly dusted with Bisquick, roll dough and knead gently, about 10 times until smooth. Roll into an oblong shape, 16 x 7 inches. Spread with softened butter; sprinkle with ¼ cup brown sugar. Roll, beginning at wide end; seal. Cut into 12 slices.

In each greased muffin cup, drop 2 teaspoons brown sugar, 2 teaspoons melted butter, 2 or 3 pecan halves. Place rolls, cut side down in muffin cups.

Bake for 10 minutes. Invert pan immediately; remove after 1 minute.

HOT CROSS BUNS

½ cup warm water
1 teaspoon sugar
2 packages yeast
1 ½ cups hot water
½ cup skim milk powder
⅓ cup brown sugar
½ cup cooking oil
2 tablespoons molasses
3 eggs
1 cup graham flour
2 cups white flour
2 cups whole wheat flour
2 teaspoons salt
2 teaspoons cinnamon }
½ teaspoon nutmeg } may be doubled
dash of cloves }
1 cup raisins
½ cup currants
½ cup candied mixed fruit, chopped

Dissolve sugar in warm water and sprinkle over yeast. Do not stir. Let stand for 10 minutes. In a large bowl beat together hot water, skim milk powder, sugar, molasses, and eggs. Stir in yeast. Stir in remaining ingredients. Turn out onto a well-floured board and knead for 10 minutes. Return to bowl; cover with waxed paper and a damp cloth. Let rise for 1 ½ hours, or until double in size.

Punch down; knead for 5 minutes; return to bowl to rise until doubled again. Punch down. Place on board and roll with rolling pin to ½ inch thickness. Cut into rounds with a cookie cutter or an inverted glass. Place on a cookie sheet and let rise until doubled. Bake at 425°F for 12 minutes — watch that bottom does not become too brown.

(When doubling this recipe increase yeast to 5 packages instead of 4.)

When cool make crosses with icing and decorate with a sliced cherry.

WALLY CROUTER'S HEALTHY AND HASTY MORNING MUFFINS

Makes 18 Muffins

Mash 4 bananas in a large mixing bowl (the riper the better)

Add:

1 cup buttermilk

1/3 cup molasses

2 eggs, well beaten

2 tablespoons margarine, melted

Beat well. Add 2 cups of unprocessed wheat bran and let stand. Turn oven on at 375°F.

In a separate bowl, *mix:*

1/2 cup gluten flour

1/2 cup whole wheat flour

1/2 cup ground walnuts

1 rounded teaspoon baking powder

1/2 teaspoon baking soda

3/4 teaspoon salt

2 handfuls of raisins

2 handfuls of chopped walnuts

10 to 15 shakes each of nutmeg and cinnamon

ADD to bran mixture. Fill well-greased muffin pans and bake for about 20 minutes, or until a good rich golden colour.

RUM CREAM PIE

Serves 8

1-9 inch baked pie shell (or crumb crust)

6 egg yolks

1 scant cup of sugar

1 tablespoon gelatine

½ cup cold water

1 pint whipping cream

½ cup light rum

shaved chocolate

Beat egg yolks until they are light and add sugar. Soak gelatine in cold water until dissolved.

Put gelatine and water over low heat and let it come to a boil; pour it over the egg and sugar mixture, stirring briskly.

Whip cream and fold it into the egg mixture; flavour it with rum. Cool and pour into prepared pie shell, refrigerate several hours.

When set, sprinkle generously with shaved chocolate curls.

TOASTED ALMOND PIE

1 unbaked pie shell (9 inch)

3 eggs

1 cup corn syrup

1 cup brown sugar

¼ teaspoon salt

1 teaspoon vanilla

1 teaspoon almond flavouring

3 tablespoons butter, melted

2 cups toasted almonds, coarsely chopped

Method:
Preheat oven to 350°F. Bake pie shell for 10 minutes. Beat eggs; add remaining ingredients. Pour into partially baked pie shell and bake at 350°F for 45 to 50 minutes.

Garnish:

¾ cup whipping cream

2 tablespoons icing sugar

2 tablespoons rum

Whip cream; blend in sugar and rum or liqueur.

MARGARET ATWOOD'S NOVA SCOTIA ROLLED OATS BROWN BREAD

Makes 2 Loaves

1 1/2 cups rolled oats

2 teaspoons salt

2 cups boiling water

1 tablespoon shortening

1 package granulated yeast

1 teaspoon sugar

1/2 cup warm water

3/4 cup table molasses

4 to 5 cups all-purpose flour

Stir oats and salt into boiling water; add shortening. Combine yeast, sugar and warm water; let stand for 10 minutes. Add molasses to oatmeal mixture; then add enough flour to make a fairly stiff dough. Add yeast mixture; mix well. Let rise in a buttered bowl, until light and double in bulk. Punch down. Pour into 2 loaf pans. Let rise again!

Bake at 350°F for 45 minutes. (I brush tops with melted butter after removing from oven.)

A family treasure.

CHOCOLATE MOUSSE PIE

Serves 8

38 chocolate wafers, crushed

1/3 cup melted butter

6 ounces chocolate chips

1 egg whole

2 eggs, separated

1 cup heavy cream, whipped

1 teaspoon light rum

Mix crushed wafers and melted butter. Blend well. Press into a buttered 9 inch pie plate. Set aside. Melt chocolate chips over hot, not boiling water. Beat in one whole egg; add egg yolks one at a time and beat well. Beat egg whites until stiff. Remove chocolate mixture from stove; fold in beaten egg whites, whipped cream and rum. Pour chocolate mixture into pie shell; chill thoroughly.

GLAZED STRAWBERRY PIE

Serves 8

3¼ ounce package vanilla pudding and pie filling

1 tablespoon Cointreau

1 quart strawberries

2/3 cup water

1 cup sugar

3 tablespoons cornstarch

1/3 cup water

red food colouring

9 inch pie shell, baked

Bake pie filling as directed; when lukewarm stir in Cointreau. Pour into baked pie shell. Wash, hull and dry berries. Save 1 cup and put remaining berries, stem end down and close together, on top of filling. Simmer remaining cup of berries and 2/3 cup water until berries break up, about 3 minutes.

Blend sugar and cornstarch and stir in 1/3 cup water until smooth. Add to boiling berries and boil, stirring, for 1 minute. Add a few drops food colouring to make a bright red. Cool but do not chill. Pour over berries in pie shell and chill until firm.

FRANK SHUSTER'S APPLE-PEAR PIE

Serves 6 to 8

Crust:

9 or 10 inch pie dish

$2\frac{1}{8}$ cups all-purpose flour

½ cup butter

½ cup shortening

½ teaspoon salt

$4\frac{1}{2}$ tablespoons cold water

Sift flour three times. Add salt. Cut in butter and shortening until pieces are the size of peas. Add water, mix until dough holds together. Handling dough as little as possible, form into a ball, divide in half and keep in refrigerator until ready to use.

Filling:

4 Spy apples (medium)

2-14 ounce cans pears, drained

juice of 1 to 2 lemons (to taste)

¼ cup flour

1 cup light brown sugar

2 tablespoons butter

Peel and slice apples; place in bowl and add lemon juice. Preheat oven to 425°F.

Roll dough out on lightly floured board. Line buttered pie plate with dough. Sprinkle with half the flour. Arrange layer of apples. Sprinkle with half the sugar and dots of butter. Add layer of sliced pears. Repeat; flour, apples, (including juice), sugar, butter, etc. piling the fruit highest in the centre. Cover with pastry pinching top and bottom dough together. Cut several slits in top pastry.

Bake about one hour, until centre is tender and crust golden brown. Serve warm with either ice cream or Cheddar cheese or both.

CREAMY LEMON PIE

Makes 3 Pies

3-9 inch pie shells

½ pint whipping cream

1-10 ounce tin condensed milk

1-6 ounce can frozen lemonade concentrate (not pink)

Bake pie shells. Cool. Whip cream, add thawed lemonade concentrate and condensed milk. Blend well and pour into pie shells. Chill or freeze for future use.
Eat one! Freeze two!

UTTERLY DEADLY PECAN PIE

Serves 8

1 cup sugar

1 ½ cups corn syrup

4 eggs

4 tablespoons butter

1 teaspoon vanilla

1 ½ cups broken pecans

1-9 inch pie shell, unbaked

Boil sugar and syrup for 2 to 3 minutes. Beat eggs. Slowly pour eggs into hot syrup. Add butter, vanilla and nuts. Turn into an unbaked pie shell. Bake at 375°F for 45 minutes.

LEMON MERINGUE PIE

Serves 8

1 baked 9 inch pie shell

½ cup lemon juice

1 teaspoon grated lemon rind

1 ⅓ cups sweetened condensed milk

2 eggs, separated

¼ teaspoon cream of tartar

4 tablespoons sugar

Combine lemon juice and grated lemon rind; gradually stir into condensed milk. Add egg yolks and stir until well blended. Pour into cooled pastry shell.
Add cream of tartar to egg whites; beat until almost stiff enough to hold peaks. Add sugar gradually, beating until stiff but not dry. Pile lightly on pie filling. Bake at 325°F until lightly browned, about 15 minutes. Cool.

COFFEE-TOFFEE PIE

Serves 6 to 8

Pastry Shell:

½ package pie crust mix

¼ cup brown sugar

¾ cup finely chopped walnuts

1 square unsweetened chocolate, grated

1 teaspoon vanilla

1 tablespoon water

Combine crumbled pie crust mix, sugar, walnuts and grated chocolate. Add 1 tablespoon water and vanilla. Using fork, mix well until blended. Turn into a greased 9 inch pie plate. Press firmly against bottom and sides of plate. Bake in 375°F oven for 15 minutes. Cool.

Filling:

½ cup soft butter

¾ cup sugar

1 square unsweetened chocolate, melted and cooled

2 teaspoons instant coffee

2 eggs

Beat butter until creamy, add sugar, chocolate and coffee. Add one egg and beat 6 minutes. Add remaining egg and beat 5 minutes. Turn filling into pie shell and refrigerate *overnight.*

Topping:

2 cups whipped cream (1 carton)

2 teaspoons instant coffee

½ cup icing sugar

Combine cream with instant coffee and sugar. Place in fridge, covered for one hour. Beat mixture until stiff. Refrigerate for at least 2 hours before serving.

PEPPERMINT ICE CREAM PIE

Serves 8 to 10

3 pints vanilla ice cream slightly softened

1/4 pound peppermint candies crushed

2 cups chocolate wafer crumbs

1/3 cup soft butter

1 cup heavy cream

1/4 cup chopped walnuts

Fudge Sauce:

3 squares unsweetened chocolate

1/2 cup water

3/4 cup sugar

1/4 teaspoon salt

4 1/2 tablespoons butter

3/4 teaspoon vanilla

Crush peppermint with a hammer or in a food processor using steel blade. Turn ice cream into a large bowl. With a spoon, swirl crushed candy into ice cream; just enough to give a marbled effect, don't over mix. Return ice cream to container. Freeze.

Combine wafer crumbs with butter: mix with fork until thoroughly combined. Press crumb mixture evenly on bottom and side of a 9 inch pie plate. Refrigerate until well chilled about 1 hour.

Fudge Sauce:
In a small saucepan, combine chocolate with water. Cook over low heat, stirring occasionally, until chocolate is melted. Add sugar and salt; cook stirring, until sugar is dissolved and mixture thickens, about 5 minutes. Remove from heat; stir in butter and vanilla. Let cool. Fill pie shell with scoops of ice cream. Pour 1/2 cup Fudge Sauce over top. Store in freezer until serving.

Just before serving, garnish with mounds of whipped cream, sprinkle with nuts. Pass rest of Fudge Sauce, if there is any left from the kitchen cooks!

A favourite of all but especially children.

CLAIRE AND FARLEY MOWAT'S OPEN FACED APPLE PIE

Serves 8

3 tablespoons butter, melted

5 cups apples, peeled and sliced

2/3 cup sugar

1 tablespoon cornstarch

1/2 teaspoon cinnamon

1 cup grated Cheddar cheese

pastry for 1-9 inch pie shell (unbaked)

Preheat oven to 425°F. Line pie plate with pastry. In a large bowl pour melted butter over apples, toss with a fork, coating apples completely. In a small bowl combine sugar, cornstarch and cinnamon. Sprinkle 1 tablespoon of this mixture over unbaked pie shell.

Add the remaining sugar-cinnamon mixture to the apples; toss with a fork; pour apples into the shell. Bake at 425°F for 30 minutes (or until apples are tender). Remove pie from oven and sprinkle cheese over apples. Return to oven for about 3 minutes, until cheese is melted. Serve warm.

GRANDMOTHER'S PIE CRUST

Enough for 2 - 9 inch Pie Shells

3 cups flour

1 teaspoon salt

½ pound shortening

1 egg

1 teaspoon vinegar

½ cup cold water

Mix all ingredients together. Refrigerate for 24 hours before using.

MANDARIN ANGEL PIE

3 egg whites

¼ teaspoon cream of tartar

1 cup sugar

1-4 ounce package lemon pudding mix

½ cup sugar

¼ cup water

3 egg yolks

1-11 ounce can mandarin orange sections

1 tablespoon lemon juice

½ cup whipping cream, whipped

Beat egg whites and cream of tartar to soft peaks. Gradually add 1 cup sugar, beating until it forms stiff peaks. Spread on bottom and sides of a well-greased 9 inch pie plate. Bake at 275°F for 1 hour. Turn off heat; let crust dry in the oven with the door closed for 2 hours. In a bowl combine the pudding mix, the ½ cup sugar and water; beat in the egg yolks.

Drain orange sections, reserving syrup. Add lemon juice and enough water to syrup to make 1¾ cups; stir into the pudding mixture. Cook and stir over medium heat until boiling. Cool completely. Fold in whipped cream and ¾ cup orange sections (set aside remainder); spoon into meringue shell. Chill several hours or overnight. Top with additional whipped cream and orange sections.

PUMPKIN PIE

Serves 8

Pastry for 2 crust 9 inch pie

5 eggs

28 ounce can pumpkin

1 1/2 cups brown sugar, packed

1/2 cup granulated sugar

1/4 cup molasses

1 1/2 cups light cream

1 teaspoon salt

3 teaspoons cinnamon

1 1/2 teaspoons nutmeg

1/2 teaspoon ginger

1/4 teaspoon cloves

4 ounce package cream cheese (room temperature)

1 tablespoon light cream

1 tablespoon molasses

Divide pastry into 2 equal pieces and use each to line a 9 inch plate building a high fluted edge to hold filling. Do not prick pastry. Preheat oven to 425°F.

Beat eggs lightly in large bowl. Stir in pumpkin, brown sugar, granulated sugar, 1/4 cup molasses, 1 1/2 cup cream, salt and spices. Beat until blended.

Pour pumpkin mixture into unbaked pie shells (about 4 cups per pie). Cover edges of crusts with narrow strip of foil to keep them from browning too much. Bake 20 minutes at 425°F. Reduce temperature to 325°F and continue baking about 35 minutes or until knife inserted about 1 inch from edges comes out clean (centre will be a little soft but will set as pie stands). Remove foil about 10 minutes before end of baking. Cool.

Blend cream cheese, 1 tablespoon light cream and 1 tablespoon molasses until fluffy. Put through an icing tube to from a lattice on top of each pie. Chill until shortly before serving.

BUTTERSCOTCH FUDGE BOILED ICING

4 or 5 tablespoons butter

1 cup brown sugar

¼ cup milk

1 ½ to 2 cups icing sugar

In a saucepan, mix together butter, brown sugar and milk; stir over medium heat for 1 minute; boil for 2 minutes more.

Add the icing sugar; bring to boil again; pour quickly over baked cake. Superb over banana cake!

Or, for a difference, pour into shallow dish, cool slightly, cut in squares and refrigerate for butterscotch fudge.

WALNUT CAKE

1 ½ cups butter

2 cups sugar

6 egg yolks, lightly beaten

¾ cup milk

¼ cup brandy

1 teaspoon vanilla

3½ cups flour

½ teaspoon salt

2 cups walnuts, coarsely chopped

6 egg whites

1 teaspoon cream of tartar

icing sugar

Cream butter. Gradually add sugar and beat together until light and fluffy. Beat in egg yolks.

In a small bowl mix together milk, brandy, and vanilla. Sift together flour and salt; add walnuts. Beat egg whites until foamy, add cream of tartar and continue beating until stiff. Fold into batter gently but thoroughly.

Pour into a greased and floured 20 cm tube pan and bake at 275°F for 2½ hours. Cool cake for 30 minutes. Remove from pan and cool completely. Sift icing sugar over top of the cake.

CARROT CAKE

Serves 12

2 cups packed brown sugar

1 1/4 cups vegetable oil

4 eggs

2 cups cake and pastry flour or all-purpose flour

2 teaspoons baking powder

2 teaspoons soda

2 teaspoons cinnamon

1 teaspoon salt

3 cups raw carrot, grated

Combine sugar and oil. Beat in eggs one at a time. In another bowl combine flour, baking powder, soda, cinnamon, salt and gradually stir into the oil mixture. Add carrots and beat approximately 100 strokes.

Grease 2 - 8 inch round cake pans, pour half the batter into each and bake at 350°F for 35 minutes.

Frosting:

4 tablespoons soft butter

8 ounces cream cheese at room temperature

1/2 teaspoon vanilla

3 cups icing sugar, sifted

Combine these ingredients and beat well. Spread frosting between layers of cake as well as outside.

COCONUT POUND CAKE

Makes 2 Cakes

10 eggs, separated

2 cups sugar

2 cups butter

1 tablespoon vanilla

4 cups flour (cake flour preferably; if all-purpose, use 3½ cups)

½ cup flaked coconut, chopped

Beat egg whites until foamy white and double in volume in a medium-sized bowl; beat in ¼ cup sugar, 1 tablespoon at a time, until meringue stands in firm peaks.

Cream butter, add remaining sugar and egg yolks; beat at high speed for 3 minutes. Add vanilla. Blend in flour until just mixed. Fold in meringue and coconut.

Pour batter into two greased loaf pans. Bake at 325°F for 1 hour and 15 minutes.

MOCHA CAKE

Serves 10 to 12

6 eggs, separated

1 cup sugar

1 tablespoon instant coffee

1 cup flour

1 teaspoon baking powder

Beat egg yolks in large bowl. Gradually add sugar and coffee. Sift flour and baking powder together, add to egg mixture all at once.

Beat egg whites until stiff, fold lightly into mixture. Pour into 2 ungreased 9 inch round pans. Bake at 350°F for 12 minutes. Cool.

Frosting:

¼ pound butter

¼ cup cocoa

¼ cup hot strong coffee

1 cup icing sugar

½ teaspoon vanilla

Filling:

½ pint whipping cream.

To prepare frosting, cream butter and gradually add sugar and cocoa. Then with a little coffee from time to time. Add vanilla. If the mixture is too thin to spread, add a little more sugar and cocoa. If too thick, add a little coffee.

Whip cream until stiff, sweeten to taste. Place one layer of cake or serving plate and frost with whipped cream. Cover with second layer and frost with icing.

KAREN KAIN'S LOW CALORIE CAFÉ AU LAIT CHEESECAKE

Serves 12

6 zwieback biscuits

½ teaspoon ground cinnamon

¼ cup cold water

2 envelopes unflavoured gelatine

½ cup boiling water

¾ cup brown sugar

¼ teaspoon salt

3 cups cream style cottage cheese

2 egg yolks

4 teaspoons instant coffee powder

1 teaspoon vanilla

2 egg whites

¼ teaspoon cream of tartar

1-14½ ounce can evaporated skim milk, chilled icy cold (1¾ cups)

Break zwieback into blender container. Add cinnamon. Blend to crumbs. Remove and set aside.

Put cold water and gelatine in blender container; let stand for a few minutes to soften. Add boiling water, brown sugar and salt to container; blend till dissolved. Add cottage cheese, egg yolks, coffee powder and vanilla to blender; blend smooth. Pour into bowl.

Beat egg whites with cream of tartar until stiff peaks form. Whip evaporated milk until soft peaks form. Fold whipped evaporated milk into gelatine mixture; fold in egg whites. Pour into 8 or 9 inch spring-form pan.

Sprinkle crumbs over cake. Chill. Only 170 calories a serving!!!

BUBBLY OATMEAL CAKE

1 1/4 cups boiling water

1 cup oatmeal (uncooked)

1/2 cup butter

1 cup sugar

1 cup firmly packed brown sugar

1 teaspoon vanilla

2 eggs

1 1/2 cups flour

1 teaspoon baking soda

1/2 teaspoon salt

3/4 teaspoon cinnamon

1/4 teaspoon nutmeg

Pour boiling water over oats; cover and let stand 20 minutes. Beat butter until creamy, gradually add sugars and beat until fluffy. Blend in vanilla and eggs. Add oatmeal mixture; mix well. Mix flour, soda, salt, cinnamon and nutmeg. Add to creamed mixture, blending well. Pour batter into well greased and floured 9 inch square pan at 350°F for 50 to 55 minutes. *Do not remove* cake from pan.

Frosting:

1/4 cup melted butter

1/2 cup firmly packed brown sugar

3 teaspoons cream

1/3 cup chopped nuts

3/4 cup shredded coconut

Combine all ingredients. Spread evenly over cake. Broil until frosting becomes bubbly. Cake may be served warm or cold.

VICTOR FELDBRILL'S YUM YUM MOCHA CAKE

Serves 8 to 10

1-10 ounce package miniature marshmallows

1 cup boiling water

4 teaspoons instant coffee

1 pint whipping cream

chocolate wafers or ladyfingers

In top of double boiler, combine marshmallows, boiling water and coffee. Stir constantly until all ingredients are melted. Refrigerate until hard (approximately 4 hours)

Whip cream until thick. Whip marshmallow mixture from refrigerator. Fold the two together.

Line 8 inch or 9 inch spring-form pan on sides and bottom with chcolate wafers or ladyfingers. Add half the mixture. Add another layer of chocolate wafers. Add the rest of the mixture.

Before serving sprinkle with chocolate shavings.

CAFÉ DU MIDI CONCORD CAKE

Makes 3 cakes
Ingredients for 1 cake in brackets

Meringue:

18 egg whites (6)

2 cups sugar (2/3 cup)

2½ cups icing sugar (7/8 cup)

10 tablespoons cocoa (3 tablespoons)

Beat egg whites until they hold soft peaks. Continue beating, adding sugar 2 to 3 tablespoons (one tablespoon) at a time until eggs hold stiff peaks. Sift in icing sugar and cocoa, fold in gently.

Pipe in 8 inch circles with large round tip onto greased and floured baking sheets to make six rounds (two rounds). Bake in 300°F oven for 1½ hours. Cool on sheets.

Mousse:

18 ounces semi-sweet chocolate (6 ounces)

1 pound butter (1/3 pound)

18 egg yolks (6 egg yolks)

23 egg whites (8 egg whites)

2½ cups sugar (7/8 cup)

Melt chocolate and butter in double boiler. Cool in refrigerator. Meanwhile beat the egg whites until they hold soft peaks then start adding sugar 2 to 3 tablespoons (1 tablespoon) at a time until they hold very stiff peaks. Stir egg yolks into cool but still liquid chocolate. Fold carefully and thoroughly into egg white mixture. Layer meringue and mousse beginning with a meringue, then mousse, then meringue and finally icing top and sides with mousse.

A few tablespoons (a tablespoon) of Grand Marnier can be added to the cool chocolate mixture if you wish. Refrigerate several hours before serving.

Cut Concord cake with a cold, wet, sharp knife and wet hands. To serve sprinkle lightly with sifted icing sugar. This is a very difficult cake to slice and serve.

London's Café du Midi's specialty — this is the first time this recipe has been given out.

CHERRY POUND CAKE

1 1/2 cups butter, or half butter, half shortening

2 cups sugar

3 eggs

3 1/2 cups all-purpose flour

1 1/2 teaspoons baking powder

1 teaspoon salt

1 cup warm milk

2 teaspoons almond flavouring

1/2 pound glacé cherries

Cream butter and add sugar. Beat in eggs one at a time.

Mix flour, salt and baking powder, and add to sugar mixture alternately with warmed milk. Add flavouring.

Chop cherries and roll lightly in a bit of flour. Add to batter and mix well. Put waxed paper on bottom of 12 inch angel cake pan. Pour batter in pan.

Put in oven at 325°F. Turn oven down to 300°F and cook for 2 hours. Cool on rack before removing from pan.

LEMON CHEESE CAKE

2 pounds cream cheese

3 tablespoons lemon juice

rind of 1 lemon finely grated

1/2 pound sugar

pinch of salt

4 egg yolks

1/2 pint whipping cream

1 1/2 tablespoons unflavoured gelatine powder

1 plain sponge cake cut in half lengthwise.

Mix cream cheese, lemon juice, rind, sugar, salt and egg yolks and whip for 10 minutes. In a separate bowl, whip cream until stiff. Stir gelatine into 1/4 cup cold water and beat until gelatine dissolves.

Add gelatine to cream cheese mixture.

Fold in whipped cream.

In ungreased spring-form pan, place one thin layer of sponge cake on bottom and cover with cream cheese mixture. Place second layer of sponge cake on top and refrigerate for 4 to 6 hours.

To serve, sprinkle with icing sugar and serve with fresh seasonal berries.

APPLESAUCE CAKE

1 cup dark brown sugar, packed

½ cup butter

1 egg

1 teaspoon vanilla

1 cup chopped nuts

1 ½ cups applesauce, fresh or canned

1 teaspoon cinnamon

2 cups flour

2 teaspoons baking powder

¼ teaspoon salt

Cream sugar and butter. Add egg and vanilla and mix well. Stir in nuts, applesauce and mixed dry ingredients.

Turn into greased loaf pan.

Bake at 350°F for 1 hour.

APPLE CAKE

Serves 4

1 cup sugar

1 cup flour

2 teaspoons baking powder

pinch of salt

3 eggs

½ cup vegetable oil

4 to 5 apples

1 teaspoon cinnamon

½ cup sugar

crushed walnuts

Preheat oven to 350°F. Mix together 1 cup sugar, flour, baking powder, and salt. Add well-beaten eggs and oil. Set aside. Pare and slice apples. Dust them with ½ cup sugar and cinnamon.

Grease an 8 x 8 inch glass pyrex dish. Into the pyrex dish spread evenly a single layer of batter; cover with a layer of sliced apples. Repeat ending with the remaining cake batter. Sprinkle with crushed walnut.

Bake at 350°F until cake tests done.

CHOCOLATE FROSTING

To cover 1 - 9 inch Square Cake

1-15 ounce can condensed milk

1 tablespoon water

1/8 teaspoon salt

1/2 teaspoon vanilla

2 squares semi-sweet chocolate

Put the milk, water and salt in the top of a double boiler and mix. Add the chocolate and cook over rapidly boiling water, stirring often, until thick (about 10 minutes). Remove from the heat; cool; stir in vanilla.

In minutes this icing is ready to frost your favourite cake.

GERMAN BEER CAKE

Serves 12 to 16

1 cup molasses

1/4 cup butter

2 eggs

1 cup beer

2 1/2 cups flour

1 cup raisins

1/2 cup walnuts, chopped

1 1/2 teaspoons baking soda

1/2 teaspoon ginger

1/2 teaspoon cinnamon

1/4 teaspoon ground cloves

1/4 teaspoon nutmeg

In a large bowl, mix molasses and butter; add eggs and beat until well-blended. Add beer alternately with flour. Stir in raisins, walnuts, baking soda and seasonings. Blend thoroughly.

Pour into a 9x13x2 inch baking dish. Bake at 350°F for 45 to 50 minutes. Remove from oven, cool and dust with icing sugar before serving.

A "ONE BOWL" CHOCOLATE CAKE

Serves 8

1-18 ounce package dark chocolate cake mix

1-6 ounce package instant chocolate pudding mix

4 eggs

1 cup sour cream

½ cup warm water

½ cup vegetable oil

Mix everything together in "a Bowl"; beat thoroughly for 5 minutes. Place in a greased Bundt pan and bake at 350°F for 55 minutes. Remove, cool, and dust with icing sugar.

This cake will keep moist for several days.

BUTTERLESS, EGGLESS, MILKLESS CAKE

Makes 1 Cake

1 cup sugar

½ cup shortening

1 cup water

1 cup raisins

¼ teaspoon nutmeg

¼ teaspoon salt

1 teaspoon ground cloves

1 teaspoon cinnamon

2 cups flour

½ teaspoon baking powder

1 teaspoon baking soda, dissolved in 1 tablespoon of hot water

½ cup chopped walnuts (optional)

Boil the first 8 ingredients together for 3 minutes. Let mixture cool. Add remaining ingredients. Mix well.

Bake at 325°F in a loaf tin for 45 minutes or until done.

TWO LAYER CHOCOLATE CAKE

Serves 8 to 10

2 cups flour

3/4 teaspoon baking soda

1/4 teaspoon salt

4 squares semi-sweet chocolate

1/3 cup boiling water

3/4 cup butter

1 1/3 cups sugar

3 eggs, separated

3/4 cup buttermilk

3/4 teaspoon vanilla

Sift together dry ingredients. Stir the chocolate and boiling water until chocolate is melted, cool.

Cream butter and sugar until fluffy. Beat egg yolks into butter mixture, one at a time. Add chocolate and vanilla. Add flour alternately with buttermilk, beating well after each addition.

Beat egg whites to stiff peaks and fold into batter. Line 2 - 9 inch cake tins with waxed paper, pour in batter and bake at 350°F for 25 to 30 minutes.

Coconut Pecan Frosting:

1 cup evaporated milk

1 cup sugar

3 egg yolks

1/2 cup butter

1 teaspoon vanilla

1/2 cup coconut

1 cup chopped pecans

Mix milk, sugar, egg yolks, butter and vanilla in saucepan. Cook over medium heat, stirring constantly for about 12 minutes until mixture thickens.

Remove from heat; add coconut and pecans. Beat until cool and of spreading consistency.

RICH RAISIN SCONES

Makes 16 to 20 Scones

2 cups sifted pastry flour

1/3 cup sugar

2 1/2 teaspoons baking powder

1/4 teaspoon baking soda

1/2 teaspoon salt

1/3 cup shortening

1/3 cup raisins

1 egg

2/3 cup commercial sour cream, approximately

Measure the once sifted flour and sift with sugar, baking powder, soda and salt. Cut in shortening finely, using pastry blender. Add raisins. Beat egg and add 1/2 cup sour cream. Add to dry mixture combining lightly with a fork. Mix in enough additional sour cream to make a dough which is soft but not sticky. Knead about 15 seconds on lightly floured surface to shape the dough. Pat into 2 1/2 inch rounds and place on greased cookie sheet. Score in quarters with a sharp knife. Sprinkle with a little nutmeg and bake at 400°F for about 20 minutes.

7

Rich Raisin Scones
Recipe on page 224

HAZELNUT TARTS

Makes 24 - 2 inch Tarts

Pastry for 24 - 2 inch tarts

2 eggs

½ cup corn syrup

½ cup sugar

1 teaspoon flour

¼ teaspoon salt

2 tablespoons butter, melted

1 cup toasted hazelnuts, coarsely chopped

Method:
Preheat oven to 400°F. Beat eggs; add remaining ingredients. Spoon into unbaked tart shells. Bake at 400°F for 5 minutes. Reduce heat to 350°F and continue baking for 15 to 20 minutes.

CHOCOLATE REFRIGERATED CAKE

Serves 8

Make the day before serving.

4 egg yolks, well beaten

2 squares unsweetened chocolate, melted

½ cup sugar

¼ cup water

1 cup butter

2 cups icing sugar

1 teaspoon vanilla

4 egg whites, beaten until stiff

2 dozen ladyfingers

whipped cream to garnish

Beat egg yolks.

Boil sugar and water for 5 minutes. Add the melted chocolate; pour mixture slowly over the beaten egg yolks. Cool. Cream butter and add icing sugar. Combine with the chocolate mixture and beat until light. Fold in stiff egg whites and add vanilla.

Line sides and bottom of mould with waxed paper and ladyfingers; add mixture. Let stand in refrigerator for 24 hours. Turn out and decorate with whipped cream.

PEACH OR PINEAPPLE UPSIDE DOWN CAKE

Serves 6 to 8

2 tablespoons butter

1/4 cup brown sugar

peaches or pineapple, canned or fresh

1 1/3 cups Tea Biscuit mix

3/4 cup sugar

3 tablespoons soft shortening

1 egg

3/4 cup milk

1 teaspoon vanilla

Melt butter in 8 inch square or 9 inch round cake pan. Sprinkle with brown sugar. Arrange fruit on top of butter and sugar.

Mix biscuit mix and sugar. Cut in shortening. Blend well. Add egg and 1/4 cup milk. Beat vigorously for 1 minute. Gradually stir in remaining milk, and vanilla. Beat 1/2 minute. Pour cake mixture over fruit. Bake 35 to 40 minutes at 350°F.

Invert at once on serving plate. Cool slightly and remove pan.

Always a favourite.

APRICOT UPSIDE DOWN CAKE

Serves 6

1/2 cup butter

1 cup sugar

2 eggs, unbeaten

2 1/4 cups cake flour, or 2 cups all-purpose flour

2 1/2 teaspoons baking powder

1/4 teaspoon salt

2/3 cup milk

1 teaspoon vanilla

brown sugar

tinned apricots

Cream butter and add sugar gradually. Add one egg at a time and beat well. Sift dry ingredients together 3 times. Add milk alternately with dry ingredients and add vanilla.

Grease bottoms of muffin tins heavily with butter. Add 1 teaspoon brown sugar and 1/2 apricots.

Fill tins 2/3 full of batter. Bake in 350°F oven for 25 minutes. Turn out at once. Serve warm with whipped cream.

DARK CHRISTMAS CAKE

2 cups seedless raisins, washed and drained

2 cups seeded raisins, separated

1 cup currants, washed and drained

1 cup slivered or chopped mixed candied peel and citron

1 cup maraschino cherries, drained and halved

1 cup almonds, blanched and halved

¾ cup grape juice or brandy

3 cups once-sifted pastry flour or 2⅔ cups once-sifted all-purpose flour

1 teaspoon baking powder

¾ teaspoon salt

2 teaspoons ground cinnamon

½ teaspoon grated nutmeg

½ teaspoon ground ginger

⅛ teaspoon ground cloves

¾ cup butter

1½ cups granulated sugar

4 eggs

¼ cup molasses

1 teaspoon vanilla

Prepare seedless raisins, seeded raisins, currants, peels, cherries and almonds; place in a bowl.

Pour grape juice or brandy over prepared fruits and nuts and combine well. Let stand overnight.

Sift the pastry or all-purpose flour, baking powder, salt, cinnamon, nutmeg, ginger and cloves together 3 times.

Cream the butter; gradually blend in sugar and cream well.

Add unbeaten eggs to the creamed mixture, one at a time, beating in well after each addition.

Beat in the molasses and vanilla.

Add half the flour mixture, combine well; add fruit, and juice mixture, combine well; add remaining flour mixture and combine well.

Turn batter into a deep 8 inch square cake pan that has been lined with a layer of aluminum foil.

Bake in a slow oven, 300°F about 2¾ hours.
Let cake stand in its pan on a cake rack until cold.
Store in a closely covered crock or tin to ripen and if desired, drizzle with brandy once a week.
Make at least six weeks before Christmas.

LEMON CAKE

Serves 8

1 package lemon cake mix

1-4 ounce package instant lemon pudding mix

¾ cup of water

¾ cup vegetable oil

4 whole eggs

Blend the dry mixes; add the water and beat well. Add the oil and beat again, until the batter is thick and glossy. Add the whole eggs, one at a time, beating after each addition and continue beating for 3 more minutes.
Pour into a well-oiled and well-floured angel cake tin. Bake at 350°F for 1 hour, until golden, firm and pulls away a little from the pan.

Glaze:
½ cup sugar and 2 tablespoons lemon juice dissolved in ½ cup orange juice. Heat until sugar is dissolved and pour over cooled cake.
This cake keeps beautifully.

LEMON CURD TARTS

Serves 12

Lemon Curd:

3 eggs

1 cup sugar

scant ¼ cup butter

rind and juice of two lemons

Beat eggs; add sugar and beat thoroughly. Put egg mixture, butter, finely grated lemon rind and juice in the top of a double boiler, over boiling water. Stir mixture constantly until thickened and smooth. This should take about 15 to 20 minutes. If lumps are in the mixture, beat them out with a whisk.
Pour into clean, warm jar and store in the refrigerator. This will keep for many weeks.

Tarts:
Fill cooked tart shells about one half full with lemon curd. Bake about 20 minutes in 400°F oven.
Serve warm or at room temperature.
Note: Lemon curd can be used as jam on buns, scones or bread. It is very rich and best made into *little* tarts and *not* pies.

CHINESE SPONGE CAKE

Serves 8

8 eggs, separated

2 teaspoons cream of tartar

1 cup sugar

¼ cup milk

½ cup oil

1 teaspoon almond extract

1 ½ cups flour

black sesame seeds

In a bowl, beat egg whites and cream of tartar until very stiff; set aside. In another bowl, beat together egg yolks, sugar, milk and oil, mixing well; then beat in flour and add almond extract. Fold egg whites into cake batter; pour into a greased and floured angel cake pan. Bake at 350°F for 50 minutes. When baked, turn onto cake rack to cool. Sprinkle top with sesame seeds.

CHOCOLATE CHIP COFFEE CAKE

½ pound butter

1 cup sugar

2 eggs

2 cups flour

2 teaspoons baking powder

1 teaspoon baking soda

1 teaspoon vanilla

Topping:

1 cup chopped nuts (almonds, walnuts, etc)

1 cup brown sugar

1 teaspoon cinnamon

1 cup semi-sweet chocolate chips

Cream butter and sugar. Beat in eggs, flour, baking powder and baking soda. Add vanilla. Mix topping.

Grease an angel food pan. Sprinkle ⅓ topping on bottom of pan; pour in ½ batter; add ⅓ more of topping; then remaining batter; top with rest of topping. Bake at 350°F for 50 minutes.

Note: This batter is very thick and has to be spread with a spatula.

DOBOS TORTE

Chocolate Frosting:

10 filberts, shelled

6 egg yolks

1 cup vanilla confectioners' sugar

½ pound butter, at room temperature

6 ounces unsweetened chocolate, melted

Cake:

6 eggs, separated

½ cup sugar

1 teaspoon vanilla

1 cup cake flour

¾ cup confectioners' sugar

1 tablespoon butter

Make frosting first. In a 400°F oven, roast filberts about 5 minutes or until their skins are easily removed; then grind them finely. Cream egg yolks with sugar until light; then slowly add pieces of butter until all is absorbed. Mix in chocolate and filberts and refrigerate until needed.

For the layers, butter six-8 inch round cake pans. Beat egg whites until firm. Beat egg yolks with vanilla and sugar until light; then slowly add flour. Beat until very smooth.

Fold in egg whites until mixture is smooth and divide batter evenly among the six pans. Bake in a 400°F oven 10 minutes; then turn layers out on a rack.

When layers are cool, pick best one and set it aside on waxed paper. Spread frosting on top of other 5 layers, stack them and frost outside of cake.

Heat confectioners' sugar and 1 tablespoon butter in a small saucepan until a deep golden colour. Pour glaze quickly over the 6th layer, spreading it evenly with a spatula. Before it hardens, use a sharp, buttered knife to cut it into as many wedges as you like (12 to 16). When it dries, put it on top of the other 5 layers and spread the frosting around the outer edge.

SOUR CREAM COFFEE CAKE

Serves 6 to 8

1/4 pound butter

1 cup sugar

2 eggs

1 cup sour cream

1 1/2 tablespoons baking powder

1 teaspoon baking soda

1 1/2 cups flour

1 teaspoon vanilla

Topping:

1/4 cup sugar

1 teaspoon cinnamon

1/2 cup chopped walnuts

Cream butter and sugar; beat in eggs, then sour cream. Sift flour, baking powder and soda before adding to mixture. Pour in vanilla and beat until smooth.

Combine topping ingredients. Into a greased spring-form tube pan pour one half of batter; sprinkle on half of topping. Repeat. Bake at 350°F for 45 minutes.

DANISH APPLE CAKE

Serves 6

1 1/2 cups chunkey applesauce, canned or homemade

1/2 teaspoon vanilla

1/2 cup butter

1/2 cup sugar

1 egg well-beaten

3/4 cup flour

1/4 teaspoon salt

1/4 teaspoon baking powder

3/4 cup slivered almonds

1 teaspoon almond extract

Add vanilla to applesauce; set aside. In a large bowl, beat butter until light and fluffy; gradually add sugar and beaten egg. Blend in flour, salt, baking powder, almonds and almond extract. Butter a deep 9 inch pie plate. Cover bottom with 1/2 the batter, pour in applesauce, cover with remaining batter. Bake at 325°F for 1 hour.

Serve warm with ice creamor or whipped cream or *for a different taste try a dollop of sour cream or yogourt.*

SOUR CREAM CAKE

Serves 8

1 egg

1 cup brown sugar, packed

1 cup commercial sour cream

¾ cup flaked coconut

2 cups sifted all-purpose flour

1 teaspoon baking soda

¼ teaspoon salt

Preheat oven to 375°F. Grease a 9 inch square pan. Beat egg. Add sugar gradually, beating well after each addition. Stir in sour cream and coconut.
Sift flour, soda and salt together into mixture and beat well. Spread batter in greased pan and bake at 375°F for 25 minutes or until top springs back when touched lightly. Cool in pan. Ice.

Caramel Icing:

1 cup brown sugar, packed

⅓ cup butter

⅓ cup milk

1 cup sifted icing sugar

Boil brown sugar, butter and milk briskly in a small saucepan, stirring constantly for 3 minutes. Cool to lukewarm. Stir in icing sugar and continue stirring until right consistency to spread.

Perfect for morning bridge group.

Pickles, Sauces, etc.

PECAN TOFFEE

½ cup pecan pieces

1 ½ cups lightly packed brown sugar

½ pound butter

3 squares semi-sweet chocolate

Butter a 9 inch square pan. Spread in pan, ½ cup pecan pieces. Mix together in heavy pan, brown sugar and butter. Cook over medium heat, stirring constantly, timing 12 minutes from the time the butter is completely melted. (Mixture will bubble most of the time.)

Pour toffee mixture quickly over the nuts in pan. Put chocolate on top immediately. The heat of the toffee will melt them. Spread the chocolate around to ice toffee.

Let cool completely or freeze. Break into chunks.

ALMOND BUTTER CRUNCH

Yields 3¼ Pounds

1 pound whole almonds, blanched

6 squares semi-sweet chocolate

6 squares unsweetened chocolate

1 pound butter

2 cups granulated sugar

6 tablespoons water

2 tablespoons corn syrup

pinch of baking soda

candy thermometer

1-11¾ inch x 17¾ inch x 1 inch pan

Blanch almonds and split each nut in half while hot. Place in a buttered pan in a 350°F oven and bake until crisp and light brown. Cool. Melt chocolate in top of a double boiler over hot, *not boiling* water.

In a heavy saucepan melt butter and sugar over low heat. Add water and corn syrup. Insert candy thermometer. Turn burner to medium-high and bring mixture to a boil, stirring occasionally, until thermometer reaches 300°F. Remove from heat, quickly stir in a pinch of baking soda.

Spread cooled nuts over pan. Cover with butter-sugar mixture; let harden. When hardened spread half the melted chocolate over the top. When hard, lift whole piece, turn over on waxed paper, and spread remaining chocolate on the second side.

A candy thermometer is a must!

ZENA CHERRY'S ICE LANTERNS

(May be produced only when temperature is below freezing)

Fill a plastic bucket, better still, more than one, with water but not brim full. Put outside during the night. Next morning (do not leave longer than eight hours) take inside.

Put thick cloth in your sink and place the pail up-side down on the cloth and lift off the pail. The bottom should be solid, so cut away a hole in the centre with a large screwdriver. Pour out the water, and the lantern is ready.

Put a votive candle in an empty caviar jar, and place in the hole. Put outside in the garden, light the candle for a holiday-time decoration.

APRICOT SAUCE

Yields 1½ Cups

1 cup pure apricot jam (no added pectin)

¼ cup dark rum

2 tablespoons water

3 to 4 tablespoons dark rum

Melt jam over moderate heat in heavy saucepan; add ¼ cup rum and the water. Force the mixture through a sieve; add 3 to 4 tablespoons rum.

Serve with ice cream.

MELBA SAUCE

2 teaspoons cornstarch

1 tablespoon water

½ cup corn syrup

½ cup currant jelly

1 package frozen raspberries

In a small saucepan, combine ingredients, in order given, mix thoroughly. Place over medium heat; stirring constantly, cook until mixture comes to a full boil. Boil about 2 minutes or until somewhat thickened and clear. Remove from heat; strain and cool.

Refrigerate in covered container for use when desired.

DESSERT FRUIT TOPPING

Serves 6

1 cup sour cream

½ cup powdered sugar

1 teaspoon grated lemon peel

1 tablespoon lemon juice

¼ teaspoon vanilla

nutmeg

Combine first five ingredients; cover and chill several hours or the day before. Sprinkle with nutmeg and spoon over fruit of your choice . . . strawberries, melon, raspberries, etc.

CHOCOLATE PEPPERMINT CREAM SAUCE

12 chocolate covered peppermints

1 cup heavy cream

1 tablespoon kirsch

Melt peppermints in a double boiler over hot water. When dissolved, stir in one cup heavy sweetened cream. Heat to boiling point and add 1 tablespoon kirsch.
Serve hot or cold. Serve over chocolate brownies or ice cream.

HOT FUDGE SAUCE

3 ounces unsweetened chocolate

1/4 cup butter

1 1/2 cups icing sugar

dash of salt

1-8 ounce can evaporated milk

1/2 teaspoon vanilla

Put all ingredients except vanilla into double boiler. Cook for 15 minutes stirring occasionally. Add vanilla and serve warm.

VANILLA CUSTARD SAUCE

Yields 1½ Cups

1 cup heavy cream

4 egg yolks

1/3 cup sugar

1 1/4 teaspoons vanilla

In a saucepan scald cream over low heat.
Beat egg yolks separately with sugar until lemon coloured. Add the cream to the eggs in a stream, stirring constantly. Transfer the mixture to a saucepan and cook over moderate heat. Stirring with a wooden spatula, until it is thickened and lightly coats the spatula. Do not boil. Add vanilla, strain the custard into a bowl, and cover with a buttered round of wax paper.
Cool to room temperature.

RED WINE JELLY

Yields 6 Jelly Jars

2 cups dry red wine

3 cups white sugar

½ bottle Certo

In a pot bring wine and sugar to a boil. Boil for 2 minutes, stirring constantly. Remove from heat; stir in Certo. Mix thoroughly. Skim, with a metal spoon, stirring occasionally for 5 minutes. Pour into sterilized jelly jars. Seal with hot paraffin.

White wine may be used to make a perfect white wine jelly. They are a lovely addition when serving cheese and crackers.

ORANGE SAUCE FOR DUCKLING

6 tablespoons currant jelly

3 tablespoons sugar

2 tablespoons lemon juice

2 tablespoons port or sherry

grated rind of 2 oranges

½ teaspoon salt

⅛ teaspoon cayenne

Heat first 3 ingredients for 5 minutes. Add rest and stir until blended.

HOT WINE SAUCE FOR GAME BIRDS

Yields 1 Cup

1 tablespoon butter

½ cup red currant jelly

pinch of cayenne pepper

juice of ½ lemon

3 cloves

½ cup port

1 tablespoon cornstarch

Simmer all the ingredients except the port and cornstarch for 5 minutes. Strain and add port. If desired a little bird gravy may also be added but first skim off as much fat as possible. Add cornstarch to thicken.

Serve hot.

MUSTARD SAUCE

Makes 2 Cups

½ cup sugar

1 tablespoon dry mustard

pinch of salt

4 eggs, beaten

1 cup vinegar

1 tablespoon butter

Mix the dry ingredients together; add beaten eggs, vinegar and butter. Stir constantly over medium heat for 15 minutes.
Delicious with ham.

BLENDER HOLLANDAISE SAUCE

Yields 1½ Cups

4 egg yolks

2 scant tablespoons fresh lemon juice

pinch of salt

dash of Tabasco

½ teaspoon dry mustard

1 cup butter

Place above ingredients, except butter, in a blender and "buzz" for about 1 minute. Just before serving, heat the butter almost to the boiling point. Pour in a steady stream into the blender mixture; blend until smooth and creamy.

BÉARNAISE SAUCE

3 shallots, chopped

½ cup vinegar

2 egg yolks

2 tablespoons cream

1 teaspoon each chives and tarragon

salt and pepper

8 tablespoons butter

Combine shallots and vinegar in small saucepan. Boil until vinegar measures 2 tablespoons. Strain into small heavy pan. Add remaining ingredients. Stir over low heat until mixture thickens. Do not boil.

RED PEPPER JELLY

Yields 12 Jelly Jars

2 cups sweet red peppers, ground in blender

5½ cups sugar

1 cup red wine vinegar, diluted (½ cup water plus ⅔ cup vinegar)

⅓ cup lemon juice

1 bottle pectin

1 Wash peppers, remove tongue, seeds and stem.
2 Finely chop; measure pulp and juice for recipe.
3 Place peppers, sugar and vinegar in kettle. Heat rapidly to boiling, stirring constantly.
4 Remove from heat; let stand for 15 minutes.
5 Reheat to boiling. Add lemon juice and boil for 2 minutes.
6 Remove from heat; add pectin. Skim, stirring occasionally for 5 minutes.
7 Pour into sterilized jars. Seal with paraffin. Let stand for 2 weeks before using.

CORN RELISH

Yields 7 to 8 Pints

1½ quarts (about 14 ears) corn, cook before cutting off ear.

1 quart cucumbers, peeled and chopped

1 quart onions, peeled and chopped

2 quarts tomatoes, peeled and chopped

3 red peppers, seeded and chopped

½ cup salt

Let vegetables and salt stand overnight. In the morning drain off liquid.

1 pint vinegar

4 cups sugar

1 teaspoon celery seed

1 teaspoon dry mustard

In a large kettle mix vinegar, sugar, celery seed and mustard, with the vegetables. Boil for one half hour. Bottle while hot in sterilized jars and seal with paraffin.
Excellent with any cold meat.

RAW CHILI SAUCE

Yields 6 to 10 ounce Jars

1 peck (8 quarts) tomatoes
6 large onions, finely chopped
1 cup salt
1 large hot red pepper, finely chopped
3 cups finely chopped celery
5 ounces mustard seed
2 pounds brown sugar
5 cups cider vinegar

Wash, skin and trim tomatoes, then dice. Mix tomatoes, onions and salt. Let stand overnight in a crock or a heavy pot. Drain thoroughly in the morning. Add pepper, celery, mustard seed, sugar and vinegar. Mix thoroughly. Pour into sterilized jars and seal with paraffin.

This zesty chili sauce is a hit with roast beef.

CHILI SAUCE

Makes approximately 10 Pints

1-6 quart basket tomatoes, washed, peeled and quartered
3 to 3½ cups sugar
1 dozen large onions, finely chopped
2 bunches celery, finely chopped
3 green peppers, finely chopped
3 hot red peppers, finely chopped
salt to taste
2 teaspoons ground cinnamon
4 cups cider vinegar
½ cup whole mixed spices (bound in a cheesecloth bag)

Put all ingredients in a large pot and cook very slowly; simmer for about 2 hours. Stir regularly to prevent burning. Seal in hot sterilized jars.

1-2-3 DILL PICKLES

Use dill sized cucumbers and 1 quart sterilized sealers.
1. into each sealer put;

1 fresh dill flower

1 teaspoon mustard seed

1 teaspoon powdered horseradish

½ garlic clove

2. Pack washed cucumbers into sealers; top each sealer with another dill flower.

3. Boil:

1 quart cider vinegar

2 quarts water

1 cup salt

Pour boiling liquid over cucumbers in sealers. Seal immediately.
Just as easy as 1-2-3!

APPLE AND TOMATO CHUTNEY

Yields 8 Pints

2 pounds apples

2 pounds tomatoes

¾ pound onions

1 clove garlic

½ pound dried fruit (raisins, apricots)

¾ pound sugar

1 tablespoon mustard seed

1 tablespoon curry powder

1 teaspoon cayenne pepper

salt to taste

1½ pints vinegar

Peel and core apples. Cook in very little water until tender and pulpy. Chop tomatoes, onions, garlic and dried fruit and add these with sugar to the apples. Tie mustard seed in pieces of muslin, add with remaining ingredients, including vinegar. Cook gently, approximately 2 hours. When chutney reaches desired consistency, bottle in sterilized jars and seal with paraffin.

MUSTARD BEAN PICKLE

Yields 6 Pints

8 cups fresh yellow beans

2 teaspoons turmeric

½ cup dry mustard

1 cup flour

1½ teaspoons salt

2 cups brown sugar

4 teaspoons celery seed

3½ cups vinegar

Cook beans in boiling, salted water until almost tender.

Mix dry ingredients with ½ cup vinegar to make a paste. Stir in remaining 3 cups vinegar. Cook stirring constantly until thick. Add beans. Cool slightly and seal in sterilized pint jars with paraffin.

FRUIT CHUTNEY

1 cup cider vinegar

1½ cups brown sugar

1½ teaspoons salt

¼ teaspoon ground chili peppers

1 teaspoon chili powder

1 teaspoon cinnamon

½ teaspoon ground black pepper

½ teaspoon ground cloves

½ teaspoon ground coriander

2 teaspoons powdered ginger

2 cloves garlic, minced

1 pound apples, diced (about 8)

1 pound prunes, sliced

½ pound dried apricots, diced

Place all ingredients in a very large kettle. Boil for 1 hour, stirring often, until tender. Cool. Seal with paraffin in sterilized jars.

CUCUMBER MUSTARD PICKLES

Yields 7 Pints

½ quart cucumbers

1 sweet red pepper, finely chopped

1 sweet green pepper, finely chopped

2 large onions, sliced

3 tablespoons salt

1 quart water

1 ½ cups sugar

¼ cup flour

1 ½ teaspoons celery seed

1 ½ teaspoons mustard seed

1 teaspoon turmeric

pinch of curry

2 cups vinegar

Pare cucumbers; cut lengthwise, then into 1 inch pieces. Place in a large crock. Add salt, onions, peppers, and water. Let stand at least 3 hours, preferably overnight. Drain well.

In a saucepan, combine dry ingredients and gradually stir in vinegar. Cook over medium heat, stirring constantly until sauce becomes smooth and thick, approximately 10 minutes. Add onions, cucumbers and peppers. Heat all to the boiling point. Pour hot into sterilized jars and seal with paraffin.

5 times this recipe yields 17 pints
4 times this recipe yields 14 pints

WHOLE GREEN TOMATO PICKLE

Yields 4 Pints

12 or 14 medium-sized green tomatoes

2 tablespoons salt

2 quarts water

1 quart white vinegar

3 pounds light brown sugar

2 tablespoons pickling spice

Peel your tomatoes. Let stand overnight in salt and water. Drain. In a large pot, bring vinegar, sugar and pickling spice to a boil. Add tomatoes; reduce heat; simmer until a fork will slip into the tomatoes easily. Remove tomatoes with a slotted spoon and place in sterilized pint jars. Boil down the syrup and pour over tomatoes. Seal with hot paraffin.

MUSTARD PICKLE

2 quarts small silverskin onions

2 quarts gherkins

2 cauliflowers, cut into small buds

10 pounds pickling salt

Peel onions, wash gherkins; prepare cauliflowers. Cover with salt brine (enough salt to float an egg). Let stand overnight. Pour off; repeat brine; let stand for another 24 hours. Drain.

Sauce:

2 quarts cider vinegar

2 tablespoons turmeric

4 tablespoons dry mustard

2 tablespoons curry powder

2 teaspoons cayenne pepper

1 cup flour

1 cup sugar

With 1 cup vinegar make a paste of dry ingredients. Add remaining vinegar. Cook until thickened, stirring constantly. Add to vegetables, mixing thoroughly. Bottle while hot in sterilized sealers and seal with paraffin.

FRUIT RELISH

Yields 6 Pints

2 hot red peppers, seeded and chopped

20 ripe tomatoes, peeled and chopped

8 peaches, peeled and chopped

8 pears, peeled and chopped

4 cups sugar

1 quart cider vinegar

2 tablespoons salt

6 large onions, peeled and chopped

2 tablespoons mixed pickling spice (in a cheesecloth bag)

In a large kettle, boil all ingredients together gently until thickened, about 2 hours. Bottle in sealers while hot and seal with paraffin.

INDIAN CURRY SAUCE

Makes 2 Cups

1 onion, finely chopped

3 tablespoons shortening

3 tablespoons curry powder

1 teaspoon salt

1/8 teaspoon coriander

1/8 teaspoon cumin seed

1/8 teaspoon dry mustard

1/8 teaspoon ginger

1/8 teaspoon mace

1/8 teaspoon cloves

1 garlic clove, crushed

1/4 cup water

1 8-ounce can tomato sauce

1 1/2 cups water

Brown onion in shortening in heavy skillet. Mix all spices except salt; add 1/4 cup water to make a thin paste. Add spices to skillet. Stir constantly to prevent burning but allow mixture to become good and brown. Add the tomato sauce, 1 1/2 cup water and salt to the skillet mixture. Blend until smooth; cover and simmer for about 3/4 hour. Add a little water occasionally as you will probably be serving the curry with rice.

This is a good recipe to double as it freezes beautifully.

Metric Conversion Tables

SIMPLE METRIC CONVERSION TABLE OF WEIGHT

Ounces (av)	1	2	3	4	5	6	7	8	9	10	11	12	13	14	15	16
Grams	28.3	56.7	85.0	113.4	141.7	170.1	198.4	226.8	255.1	283.5	311.8	340.2	368.5	396.9	425.2	453.6*
Pounds	1	2	3	4	5	6	7	8	9	10						
Kilograms	0.45	0.91	1.36	1.81	2.27	2.72	3.18	3.63	4.08	4.54						

SIMPLE METRIC CONVERSION TABLE OF VOLUME

Ounces (fl.)	1	2	3	4	5	6	7	8	9	10	11	12	13	14	15	16
Millilitres	28.4	56.8	85.2	113.7	142.1	170.5	198.9	227.3	255.7	284.1	312.5	341.0	369.4	397.8	426.2	454.6
Ounces (fl.)	17	18	19	20												
Millilitres	483.0	511.4	539.8	568.3(approx. 0.57 *l*)												
Pints	1	2	3	4	5	6	7	8	9	10						
Litres	0.57	1.14	1.70	2.27	2.84	3.41	3.98	4.55	5.11	5.68						
Gallons	1	2	3	4	5	6	7	8	9	10						
Litres	4.5	9.1	13.6	18.2	22.7	27.3	31.8	36.4	40.9	45.5						

SIMPLE CONVERSION TABLE OF TEMPERATURE

Degrees Fahrenheit	0	10	20	30	32*	40	50	60	70	80	90	100	200	212	400
Degrees Celsius	−17.8	−12.2	−6.7	−1.1	0*	4.4	10.0	15.6	21.1†	26.7	32.2	37.8	93.3	100.0	204.4‡

* (Water Freezes)
† (Room Temperature)
‡ (Hot Oven)

Ingredient Substitutions and Equivalents

If you don't have this . . .	you can use this
WHEN RECIPE CALLS FOR:	YOU CAN USE:
1 whole egg	2 egg yolks plus 1 tablespoon water
1 cup homogenized milk	1 cup skim milk plus 2 tablespoons butter or margarine or ½ cup evaporated milk plus ½ cup water
1 ounce unsweetened chocolate	3 tablespoons cocoa powder plus 1 tablespoon butter or margarine
1 teaspoon baking powder	½ teaspoon cream of tartar plus ½ teaspoon baking soda
1 cup sifted cake flour	7/8 cup sifted all-purpose flour
1 cup soured milk or buttermilk	1 tablespoon white vinegar plus sweet milk to equal 1 cup
1 cup sour cream	1 tablespoon lemon juice plus evaporated milk to make 1 cup
1½ teaspoons grated lemon peel	1 medium-sized lemon
2 tablespoons lemon juice	1 medium-sized lemon
3 teaspoons grated orange peel	1 medium-sized orange
4 cups sliced apples	4 medium-sized apples
1 cup egg whites	6 or 7 large eggs
1 cup egg yolks	11 or 12 large eggs
4 cups chopped walnuts or pecans	1 pound shelled walnuts or pecans

Index